CW01238622

Praise for *Rule Based Investing*

"This excellent book presents very clear and understandable rules for mitigating the risks on investments designed to earn the risk premiums on volatility and 'carry' portfolios. As well known in academia and industry, a naïve strategy of mechanically entering these investments offers a steady stream of small positive returns with occasional disastrously large negative returns. The book presents clear-cut, understandable, and sound sets of rules for attenuating the disasters but still earning nice average returns over time per unit risk. The book is quite suitable for undergraduate and master's level courses. It should also be a convenient reference and practical guide for academics and practitioners. The tables and figures are up to date, easy to read, and accompanied by a nice plain language narrative. Ms. Hsu's extensive academic and industry experience makes her a superb choice to write a book like this one."

—**George Tauchen**, Glasson Professor of Economics, Duke University

"In this challenging environment of low rates and fears of over-allocating to equities, investing professionals will be extremely interested in the strategies that Ms. Hsu has developed and refined over many years of working with sophisticated institutional clients. Her guiding principle, of earning risk premiums while protecting against large drawdowns, is simple, powerful, and persuasive. I expect that the strategies in this book, while not for the faint of heart, will improve the risk-adjusted performance of many professionally-managed portfolios."

—**Bruce Tuckman**, Clinical Professor of Finance, NYU Stern School of Business, and author of *Fixed Income Securities*.

"In *Rule Based Investing*, Chiente Hsu seamlessly blends rigorous academic theory and practical market knowledge. This is a uniquely informative and highly readable book on systematic trading strategies for modern markets."

—**Vineer Bhansali**, Managing Director and Portfolio Manager, PIMCO

"We finally have a compendium to unveil the arcane ways of systematic, rule based investment. In this book, Dr. Chiente Hsu walks the reader through a model portfolio with three independent rules based strategies. In doing so, she touches upon financial concepts, such as diversification, insurance premium, volatility, tail risk, transaction costs, liquidity, carry, and momentum, with a pragmatism that testifies to years of market practice distilled by academic knowledge. This is achieved with simplicity and transparency. Sophisticated investors willing to learn about rule based investment will particularly enjoy it."

—**Marcelo F. L. Castro**, Partner and Portfolio Manager, Pharo Management

"During the financial collapse of 2008, many systematic/quantitative investment approaches collapsed as volatility and correlations rose against them. Dr. Hsu demonstrates a variety of systematic strategies across different asset classes that have proved their resilience since the beginning of the millennium through different market conditions, in an easy to understand and pragmatic way. This book is invaluable to students and financial practitioners who want to investigate the quantitative side of investing."

—**Andy Warwick**, Managing Director and Portfolio Manager, BlackRock

"*Rule Based Investing* endeavors to be a practical manual for serious investors seeking to tap essential systematic investment strategies to diversify and enhance portfolio results. Not only does the book exceed all expectations in this regard, but it places itself at the vanguard of the practical revolution sweeping the alternative investment space right now: systematic diversification across non-correlated, rule based trading strategies can be far superior, more transparent, and *cheaper* than elliptically described and mysterious alpha strategies hawked by hedge fund gurus. With precision, clarity and accessibility to 'non-quants,' Hsu lays out how rule based strategies achieve excess returns, why there is a role for such strategies in the market, and why rule-based investing's excess returns will be sustainable in the future. Hsu masterfully combines intuitive illustrations, fundamental investment reasoning, and empirical analysis to explain key concepts and strategies. She convincingly makes the case that this exciting approach to investing provides an important edge for portfolio managers seeking excess returns."

—**Jim Conklin**, Co-CIO and Director of Research, QFS Asset Management

"In this enjoyable and readable text, Chiente Hsu explores the idea of letting a set of rules dictate exit of various strategies collecting risk premia in various corners of the market. This exit discipline already can go a long way, even before applying judgment, because it helps in the most important decision of investment: when to not be involved. *If you are successful at avoiding crisis* (when diversification fails), she goes on to show how you are left with the periods where it works very well indeed."

—**Jean-Marc Bottazzi**, Partner, Capula

"Chiente Hsu has a unique perspective that blends quantitative discipline with practical reasoning. She lays out the simple rules for investing in a clinical approach that avoids the emotional entrapment of the market. Dr. Hsu not only explains fear in the market—she demonstrates how to profit from it. A must read for any investor."

—**Molly Duffy**, Managing Director, Credit Suisse

"Chiente does an excellent job distilling complex quant strategies into simple rules. From idea formation to risk management to trade implementation, the book provides a valuable framework for developing investment strategies that should benefit both discretionary investors and quants."

—**Jia Ye**, Partner, First Quadrant

"*Rule Based Investing* is a remarkable book that allows non-experts to understand key market topics such as volatility, carry or momentum strategy. All these issues are covered in a simple and readable fashion without using complicated models and equations."

—**Stefano Natella**, Co-Head Global Secuturities Research and Analytics, Credit Suisse

"Chiente Hsu's *Rule Based Investing* will be of great help to many investors, portfolio managers, and traders. I worked closely with Chiente. She always impressed some of the world's largest asset managers and their decision makers about her quantitative approach. It was a great pleasure and honor to have worked with Chiente, a true professional in a very complex world of creating true alpha and performance."

—**Martin Wiedmann**, Global Head of FX Sales & Distribution Credit Suisse (2008-2012)

Rule Based Investing

Rule Based Investing

Designing Effective Quantitative Strategies for Foreign Exchange, Interest Rates, Emerging Markets, Equity Indices, and Volatility

Chiente Hsu

Vice President, Publisher: Tim Moore
Associate Publisher and Director of Marketing: Amy Neidlinger
Executive Editor/Acquisitions Editor: Jeanne Glasser Levine
Development Editor: Natasha Torres
Operations Specialist: Jodi Kemper
Marketing Managers: Megan Graue, Lisa Loftus
Cover Designer: Chuti Prasertsith
Managing Editor: Kristy Hart
Project Editor: Katie Matejka
Copy Editor: Language Logistics, Chrissy White; Barbara Hacha
Proofreader: Jess DeGabriele
Indexer: Tim Wright
Compositor: Nonie Ratcliff
Manufacturing Buyer: Dan Uhrig

© 2014 by Pearson Education, Inc.

Publishing as FT Press

Upper Saddle River, New Jersey 07458

This book is sold with the understanding that neither the author nor the publisher is engaged in rendering legal, accounting, or other professional services or advice by publishing this book. Each individual situation is unique. Thus, if legal or financial advice or other expert assistance is required in a specific situation, the services of a competent professional should be sought to ensure that the situation has been evaluated carefully and appropriately. The author and the publisher disclaim any liability, loss, or risk resulting directly or indirectly, from the use or application of any of the contents of this book.

FT Press offers excellent discounts on this book when ordered in quantity for bulk purchases or special sales. For more information, please contact U.S. Corporate and Government Sales, 1-800-382-3419, corpsales@pearsontechgroup.com. For sales outside the U.S., please contact International Sales at international@pearsoned.com.

Company and product names mentioned herein are the trademarks or registered trademarks of their respective owners.

All rights reserved. No part of this book may be reproduced, in any form or by any means, without permission in writing from the publisher.

Printed in the United States of America

First Printing December 2013

ISBN-10: 0-13-335434-2
ISBN-13: 978-0-13-335434-8

Pearson Education LTD.
Pearson Education Australia PTY, Limited.
Pearson Education Singapore, Pte. Ltd.
Pearson Education Asia, Ltd.
Pearson Education Canada, Ltd.
Pearson Educación de Mexico, S.A. de C.V.
Pearson Education—Japan
Pearson Education Malaysia, Pte. Ltd.

Library of Congress Control Number: 2013951005

*This book is dedicated to
Maeya, Nalla, and Nicolas.*

Contents

Introduction 1

Chapter 1 Rule Based Volatility Investment 9
    Learning to Love Volatility 9
        Volatility in Capital Markets 13
        Investing in Volatility Through Rules 17
        Profiting from Volatility and Awareness
        of the Danger 19
        The Examples of Rule Based Vol
        Investments 26
        Building a Volatility Portfolio 68
        Some Remarks 76

Chapter 2 Rule Based Carry and Momentum Investment 79
    Rule Based Carry Investment 79
        "Benchmark" Returns in the FX
        Carry Trade 83
        The Risks of the FX Carry Trade 89
        The Steam Roller 89
        Simple yet Effective Rules for
        Carry Investment 94
        Some Remarks 107

Chapter 3 Rule Based Value Investment 109
    Value in Emerging Markets 109
    Value Investing in Emerging Market FX 115
        Rule Based Investment in Emerging
        Market FX 118
    Fundamental Rules 121
        Technical Rules: Overlaying Credit
        Default Swap Spread as Market Indicator 126
        Combining Fundamental Rules
        and Risk Indicators 130

	Value Investing in Emerging Market Sovereign Bonds	134
	Fundamental Rules	135
	Technical Rules	139
	Combination of Macro Fundamentals and Market Indicator	141
	Some Remarks	147
Chapter 4	Rule Based Portfolio	149
	The Next Crisis and Beyond	157
	Bibliography	161
	Index	165

Acknowledgments

I wish to thank Bruce Tuckman, without whom this book would not be possible. Bruce has been my mentor since day one of my investment banking career. From Bruce I learned not to sacrifice intellect or morals in the fast moving world of finance.

I wish to thank George Tauchen from whom I've learned financial econometrics, and I continue learning from him. All mistakes in the book of course are my responsibility alone.

I wish to thank my colleagues and teammates at Credit Suisse. I was fortunate to be given the support and vote of confidence to run a quant team full of hard working talent.

I wish to thanks Adam Esperidiao, a brilliant inventor and entrepreneur. Adam has been key in making technical subjects accessible to a broad public audience. I look forward to our continued collaboration.

Finally, I wish to thank my husband Nicolas Sagna, whose unconditional love makes me the luckiest person and blesses my life.

About the Author

Chiente Hsu (New York, NY) is the founder of Alpha System Advisors, LLC. She was Managing Director and global head of Alpha Strategies at Credit Suisse. From 1998 to 2012, she led a team of Ph.Ds implementing quantitative investment strategies for investors, which included asset management, pension funds, corporates and hedge funds. Dr. Hsu was previously a professor at the University of Vienna, Austria, and a visiting professor at Duke University in North Carolina, teaching and conducting research in financial econometrics. She has published widely in major finance and economics journals, such as *The Review of Economics and Statistics*. Dr. Hsu holds an MA in Computer Science and Business Management from the Technical University Vienna and a Ph.D in Economics from the University of Vienna, Austria.

Introduction

"Before a person studies Zen, mountains are mountains and waters are waters; after a first glimpse into the truth of Zen, mountains are no longer mountains and waters are not waters; after enlightenment, mountains are once again mountains and waters once again waters."—Ch'ing-yüan Wei-hsin

The purpose of this book is to rediscover simple, scientifically sound investing. It has taken me the better part of my adult life spent designing and implementing complex trading strategies, both in academia and on Wall Street, to recognize simplicity. Years spent studying trades that consistently make money reveal simple truths behind their success, essential rules that winning strategies follow. More important than the intricacies of the models or parameters used, are certain fundamental principles we reduce to essential questions: Do we understand the source of the persistent returns? How do we decide when to take risk? Does the model take into account price history? Are forward-looking indicators filtering the trading decisions? Are we maximizing diversification?

Experience teaches that market expertise only goes so far, and a simple strategy broadly applied across diverse uncorrelated markets provides better protection against crisis events. Having analyzed reams of market data as only fellow "quants" can understand, we avoid the perils of "data mining" with simple "risk on/risk off" rules, sparing use of historical data and real-time indicators of market sentiment. Investors have long been told to simply "buy and hold" stock indices, that it's impossible to time the market, and that the trading fees alone would bleed you dry.

The truth is in the middle. "Buy-and-hold" is a simple yet risky strategy that experiences losses during crisis events. A trading strategy that is revisited monthly does not incur the excessive costs that doom "day trading" and is much more reactive to market realities and changes than a completely passive strategy of buy and forget. It is impossible to time market highs and lows, but it is possible as well as extremely prudent to gauge market anxieties and turn risk off when trouble threatens. The profound improvement produced by applying these rules might seem like voodoo or a glitch unique to the historical data ("fool's gold" from data mining), but it comes from extending to the financial market the same intuition we practice in everyday life. If the weather is overcast and cloudy, it does not guarantee a storm is coming, yet all the same, why take the risk of sailing on that day?

Arriving at this perspective required the accumulation of enormous human capital in the form of collaboration with many Ph.D.s over the years. In these think tanks of professionals with strong academic backgrounds, we sought always a firm grounding for why a trade makes money as well as the question of how much money it can make. Throughout my career I've continued to follow academic research to provide a better understanding of the science behind investing, drawing from theory before putting a strategy into practice in managing assets. Science moves forward from a combination of theory and practice: It is the work of theoretical physicists that informs experimental physicists "where to look" for interesting results in the natural world. We can view finance in the same light, drawing from academia the fresh ideas that inform better models and strategies. The final product of this knowledge and experience is a rule based framework of principles easily translated across asset classes for maximum diversification.

From simple rules profound changes arise. The improving safety record of the aviation industry arose after the application of rules and checklists for inspections and safety procedures before takeoff and landing. Improved metrological science keeps planes grounded when the threat of severe weather arises. Equally in medicine, implementing rules and checklists for sanitization and sterilization of hands and tools prior to surgery profoundly reduced incidents of infection once considered a natural part of healing. Through basic boilerplater investment advice, investors are taught that the "buy-and-hold" strategy is best, that the S&P 500 is the ultimate benchmark, and that there is no alternative but to accept heavy losses during crisis events—all of which are insufficient in light of rule based strategies.

You might be skeptical that if something so simple is so effective, why isn't this already widely known? Just as consumer goods are designed with a limited useful life, a "planned obsolescence" where products fail or become unfashionable after a few years, the financial industry benefits from obfuscation. In the financial world seldom is anything described as "simple"; from the industry jargon to the information overload of stock tickers, the financial industry is a cloistered world. Behind the groomed esotericism is the suggestion that those within the industry are privy to secrets others are not.

Fortunately this book is accessible not only to financial professionals, but anyone with an interest in objective rule based investing styles. Throughout the text, technical discussions of equations are avoided as much as possible (they are available, however, in the bibliography for those interested), and the focus instead is on building the intuition that informs a rule based system. The purpose of this book is to demonstrate to investors that simple rules, when built on sound scientific principles and divorced from emotions, are capable of notable results.

In the financial world it is difficult to differentiate good advice from mediocre advice from utterly incorrect advice. The bar for "decent returns" is typically considered to be the S&P 500. This intuitive faith that equity indices progressively reach ever new highs is an example of the phenomenon of *persistent returns*. It is true that in the long term indices grow because the population is growing, businesses are becoming more efficient and more innovative everyday, and opportunities continue to multiply. Civilization is generally a cycle of positive reinforcement and improvement.

The issue is then how to best capture that persistent return. The buy-and-hold strategy can work in the long run, but it is a risky strategy with volatile returns and significant exposure to extreme market events. In looking to move beyond buy-and-hold, there have been many suggestions and theories, often complicated and without grounding, of finding patterns in historical data to predict future movement. That would be an example of data mining, as it is easy to find patterns in existing data that are irrelevant to predicting future price movements.

There are other examples of markets exhibiting persistent returns that we explore together in assembling a globally diverse rule based portfolio. In volatility markets we take a look at how receiving volatility premium is a consistently profitable position analogous to the long-term success of insurance companies. Emerging market economies exhibit strong growth as revealed by GDP growth and other economic measure, which are better captured through currencies and bonds rather than equity markets. Rules are discussed for improving the carry trade among G10 currencies.

Moving beyond passive investment and the perils of data mining, you learn that you must take historical data into account only to a limited first-order degree. In the case of volatility investing, an intelligent measure of the moving average, GARCH, is used as a rule for filtering risk. In the currency carry investing, diversification is the key to persistent returns, and in value investing a ranking of macroeconomic fundamentals is used to determine the "value" of emerging market countries.

Investment decisions are further filtered by forward-looking market indicators. For the carry trade and volatility investing, you learn to use the VIX, the "fear barometer" of the market, to gauge the anxiety level over future months. In interest rates you can use the shape of the volatility curve to establish forward-looking rules. In emerging markets you can use real-time information from the credit default swap (CDS) markets to determine the market's current view of a country's credit worthiness.

The philosophy of the rules is the same: History, in the form of statistics, provides relevant background information that is further refined by the forward-looking information of market prices (such as the VIX, slope of the volatility curve, and CDS spreads). Technical rules derived from price action only are vital, but fundamental economics are not dead, as you discover in this book's discussion of value investing rules. The most powerful rules, as is demonstrated throughout, are produced by combining both historical and forward-looking filters. The strength of the complete portfolio assembled here is scientifically founded in the diversification provided by widely different asset classes. Risk is spread out among markets as unique from each other as G10 currencies, emerging market bonds, and volatility markets. Risk is spread out via distinct investment styles such as volatility, carry, and value investment. Not only do the returns of the sample portfolio provided in this book dwarf those of equity markets, the volatility is remarkably low, making for intelligent and profitable investments.

Throughout the book you are given examples based on similar investment guidelines, such as low frequency trading, where you revisit your investment decisions on a monthly basis, minimizing the concern of transaction costs. The investments to take on are long-term profitable and well understood in exhibiting a persistent premium, such as volatility premium, carry premium, and emerging market growth. There's no getting away from the fact there is potential danger in these investments, such as severe losses during a market crisis event, and you learn how to use forward-looking market prices in the forms of VIX, credit default swap spreads, or the shape of the volatility curve to filter out the worst of these events and reduce their impact. The market indicators alert you to heightened fears of potential turmoil, and during those months you should reduce risk rather than gamble on the outcome of extreme events.

After years spent in academia researching Financial Econometrics, followed by 15 years in investment banking developing quantitative investment strategies, the end result of having designed countless financial models and trading programs has been to revisit the basics of investment with a new set of eyes that recognize the salience of simple truths expressed in simple rules. To quote T.S. Eliot, *"We shall not cease from exploration / And the end of all our exploring / Will be to arrive where we started / And know the place for the first time."* These insights into a new rule based system of investing are the crystallization of my professional experience, derived from the certainty that avoiding emotion-driven decisions through informed and scientific rules produces the best and most intelligent long-term investments.

This book only scratches the surface of rule based strategies through a few examples. There are many other investment possibilities, and every day the number grows as academic research helps us to understand market interactions and causalities that lead to the design of better and more robust rules. Exciting examples mentioned here use model free volatility/variance premium to predict future returns as well as research that aims to explain and price the carry risk premium. The strategies introduced in this text can be refined for greater effectiveness as well as expanded to cover additional asset classes and markets. Furthermore, in the future publications I hope to explore to a greater depth the ability of rule based systems to signal and hedge against rare and dreaded "black swan" events.

The simplicity of these rules is also a humble acknowledgement of the unknowable chaos that churns the tides of the financial markets. How we choose to "ride the chaos" so to speak, is a challenge we must approach from the perspective of a surfer. Surfing is, after all, an apt representation of individual grace and control while balanced on the edge of the unfathomable turbulence that fathers big waves.

Inexperienced surfers are liable to exhaust themselves in a futile chase after every minor ripple that comes along, not unlike day traders, while still others, afraid of engaging the water might drift about passively behind the breakers to no avail. A seasoned surfer, however, is informed by both his ingrained experience of the beach as well as by keeping sharp eye always on the horizon, filtering out dozens if not hundreds of potential swells before the ideal wave is chosen. With the right wave selected, disciplined muscles engage, and from a sea of unpredictability there arises a graceful figure sailing the crest of foaming waters. A wise surfer is one who has learned that when bad weather threatens out in the distance, whether there will actually be a storm or not, he watches the ocean from the shore that day. Basic and intuitive truths reveal themselves in the simplest rules.

1

Rule Based Volatility Investment

Learning to Love Volatility

"Investing in volatility" might seem a contradictory phrase. Semantically we tend to equate volatility with unpredictability and chaos, precisely the abstract forces that foil most investment strategies. It is not intuitive to think of volatility as something innately valuable, nor to recognize volatility as a rich and unique asset class. Even many experienced financial professionals comfortable reading an earnings report think of volatility markets as an esoteric technical subject better left to options traders. Underlying complex mathematical pricing models, however, are intuitive market principles that explain why a "volatility premium" exists and how it can greatly benefit most portfolios.

Stocks are commonly understood as owning a share of a company, treasuries as a loan to the government, and commodities as durable physical goods, but what is the underlying value of volatility? Before investing in volatility, it's crucial to understand on a fundamental level where the potential profit comes from and why. Volatility and options are already subjects that are unfamiliar and intimidating to many, and there's no shortage of options traders and fund managers who will default to explanations involving the Black Scholes model and Greek variables of options trading. The result is the impression that making money through volatility is on par with theoretical physics rather than the application of basic market principles. Understanding that heat will spread through a spoon from one end to the other does not require solving the heat diffusion equations. Visualizing space-time as a stretched blanket in which masses such as planets cause a sag doesn't demand a doctoral degree. Equally understanding that, on average, selling volatility is a profitable strategy requires only the recognition that investors will always be willing to pay for protection against uncertainty.

The "volatility premium" exists because of investor fear. The origins of futures exchanges began with farmers seeking protection from commodity price swings through future contracts. The farmer is guaranteed a fixed price for his harvest months in advance. The speculator receives the unknown "floating" price of the harvest at a future date. The speculator stands to profit if on the contract date the market price is above the strike price and stands to lose if otherwise. This simple arrangement is no different in essence than a *volatility swap* where the "fixed price" is the implied volatility (market expectation) on the date of the swap, and the "floating price" is the actual volatility at a future date.

The contract between the farmer and speculator, however, is biased in favor of the speculator. On average, the speculators necessarily must profit more often than they lose; otherwise, they would drive themselves out of business quickly. The speculator must be paid to hold the risk and bear the uncertainty; accordingly, the farmer naturally enters the contract at a loss compared to what he would typically receive on average. In exchange for paying the speculator a premium over the long term, the farmer can sleep well at night, unafraid of possible ruin due to freak market prices. The speculator may suffer heavy losses during a bad year, but the cumulative effect of receiving the premium will in the long term more than cover such losses so that, on average, speculation remains a profitable business. "Speculator," however, is a loaded term that suggests recklessness and greed, but after speculators mature, grow, diversify, and hone their craft to a science, we call it something that sounds much more respectable: insurance.

Insurance is a familiar point of reference from which to draw informative parallels. All insurance premiums are biased toward insurance companies. Even a healthy eighteen-year-old, quoted what seems like a pittance for a generous life insurance policy, is overpaying from a risk-return perspective. Policy holders recognize that imbued in the price of a policy is not only the statistically expected rate of payout, but also all the overhead, salaries, advertising, and profit that an insurance company is required to generate. The insurance premium means that the "implied risk" of fire, accident, or death, usually exceeds the actual risk of these catastrophes occurring to policy holders. If this weren't the case, there would be no profit in insurance, and insurers would cease to exist.

Financial markets are merely an extension of these familiar principles, and with the example of overpaying for insurance premiums in mind, it shouldn't come as a surprise that market expected "implied volatility" is a biased estimate of future realized volatility. Imbued in the implied volatility price, which is a snapshot of what the market expects future volatility will be, is the volatility risk premium, which is the compensation given in exchange for bearing the risks of an uncertain future.

The risk premium exists throughout asset classes and different markets. In bond markets, long-dated bonds typically yield more than shorter-dated bonds due to the uncertainty of the future. Investors willing to take on the risk of long-dated debt are compensated by this premium because default is always possible. Credit defaults and downgrades do occur in credit markets; however, they occur less frequently than the implied default rate reflects. The implied risk of default overshoots the actual risk because the market demands a "risk premium" to be priced in for the additional uncertainty.

Furthermore, the persistence of the volatility risk premium also may be rooted in a natural imbalance in supply and demand. To return to our crutch of insurance, whereas much of the population desires insurance coverage, few are in a position to issue policies. The downside of issuing insurance policies is vast. Without deep capitalization and a broad diversified customer base, it is a recipe for disaster. In the financial markets, most participants involved in options are natural buyers, analogous to policy holders. They are using options to hedge their risks, or if they are speculating, they are doing so with the limited downside buying an option provides. On the other hand, selling options is regarded as much more dangerous because the downside is unlimited. A stock's value can drop only as low as zero, but it can increase without limit, which means an option seller can potentially experience uncapped losses. With the increased capital requirements and lower tolerance of leverage that exists after the 2008 crisis, fewer players are willing to sell options.

This imbalance is particularly sharp immediately after a market crisis, which is precisely why the aftermath of a market event is an excellent opportunity for volatility investors. Suppose we are in the business of issuing flood insurance policies in the northeast. Typically, it is a profitable business with occasional payouts that are eclipsed by the premiums we receive. Suddenly, a hundred-year storm occurs, flooding tens of thousands of houses. As insurers we suffer heavily and immediately raise premiums to account for the new realities. Following the hurricane, there will be a surge of demand for more flood insurance policies by the residents now afraid of the next storm, yet the supply of insurers willing to issue policies will shrink because they've seen what can happen and don't want to expose themselves to such drastic potential losses. High demand and low supply will produce skyrocketing flood-insurance rates in the immediate aftermath. Has the likelihood of freak weather occurrences actually increased? No. A hundred-year storm is still a hundred-year storm, as evidenced by the geological record. Logically speaking, flood insurance rates should remain unchanged, yet structural imbalances in market psychology drive pricing more than reason. The trauma of the last storm is still visceral both to homeowners who demand protection and insurers who are afraid to provide it. Contrary to our natural intuition and emotions, the best time to issue flood insurance is immediately after a crisis because that is when the risk premium is highest. In fact, after a major market crisis, volatility tends to be the best-performing asset class.

Volatility in Capital Markets

Having discussed the general principles behind volatility and risk premiums, let's now focus on how volatility is treated and utilized in capital markets. Technically speaking, *volatility* measures the magnitude of how a price changes over a specific period of time. It is widely agreed by academics and practitioners that volatility should be measured in rates of returns; that is, percentage changes in prices. The most commonly used measure of return volatility is the standard deviation measuring the dispersion of returns. *Standard deviation* summarizes the probability of extreme values occurring. For example, if X Corp stock moves up 10% one year and down 10% the next year for a decade, it has an annualized volatility of 10%. If Y Corp moves 20% up and 20% down on alternating years for a decade, it has a volatility of 20%. Even though both stock prices might end the decade unchanged from where they began, Y Corp is twice as volatile. If both X Corp and Y Corp have an average rate of return, say 10% per year, X Corp is more desirable than Y Corp because of greater price stability. X Corp stock is considered a superior investment because less risk is involved in generating the same return as Y Corp stock.

When volatility is high, the chance of large positive or negative returns is high. Mathematically speaking, the volatility of X Corp stock means that there is a 95% probability (two standard deviations) that the stock price moves between -10% and 30%. For Y Corp there is a 95% probability of the stock price moving between -30% and 40%. Granted, this assumes a normal distribution, but in reality the neat statistical principles of standard deviation are insufficient as a measure of risk, particularly for strategies with embedded tail risks (meaning when extreme events occur, it causes a disproportionately large effect in returns).

With this basic understanding, let's assume the market implies that X Corp is going to be moving an average of 10% over the next year, so implied volatility is 10%. Your research and forecast is that actual volatility will be much lower than 10%. You go "short" volatility, meaning you receive the implied volatility of 10% and will pay the realized volatility, whatever it may be. In effect, you have sold an insurance policy to people afraid of volatility over 10% occurring. If indeed it turns out that X Corp moves less than 10%, you profit. Just as the value of a stock can be researched and an investment made on whether it should increase or decrease, you can form a market view on volatility alone, separate from the direction of the price, either through qualitative assessments or quantitative models.

To use an example from the currency markets, suppose that the market is pricing that over the next year, the exchange rate of U.S. Dollar against Japanese Yen, USDJPY, has a volatility of 30% (its historical average being 15%). In contrast, your view is that the market is going to be calmer. You therefore enter a contract in which, at the end of the year, you will pay a notional value of $1,000 multiplied by the upcoming actual volatility. In return you will receive a notional value of $1,000 times the fixed volatility of 30%. At the end of the year, if actual volatility was 20%, your profit is calculated by multiplying your net 10 volatility points by $1000 each, which is $10,000 (minus transaction costs)!

Figure 1-1 illustrates how a volatility swap contract works. The same mechanism applies to a variance swap, variance being the square of volatility.

How Volatility/Variance Swap works

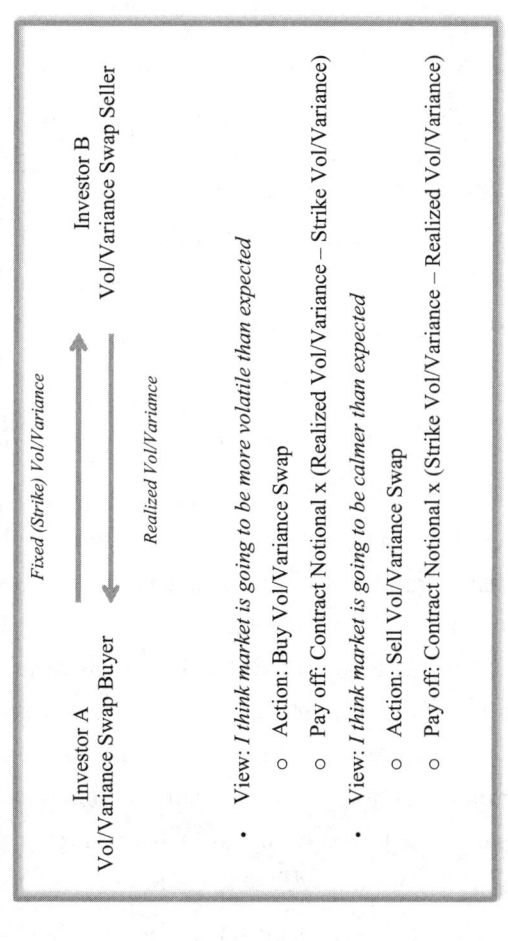

Investor A   Investor B
Vol/Variance Swap Buyer   Vol/Variance Swap Seller

Fixed (Strike) Vol/Variance

Realized Vol/Variance

- View: *I think market is going to be more volatile than expected*
  - Action: Buy Vol/Variance Swap
  - Pay off: Contract Notional x (Realized Vol/Variance − Strike Vol/Variance)
- View: *I think market is going to be calmer than expected*
  - Action: Sell Vol/Variance Swap
  - Pay off: Contract Notional x (Strike Vol/Variance − Realized Vol/Variance)

Figure 1-1 How volatility/variance swap works

It is also important to clarify what people in finance mean when they discuss volatility. If an investment strategy involves the term *vol*, the first thing to clarify is whether it is one of the following:

- **Historical volatility:** This is the standard deviation of past rate of returns, taken from price history and which often serves as an "estimate" of the unobserved actual volatility.
- **Actual volatility:** This is the volatility you want to forecast at a future time.
- **Implied volatility:** Simply speaking, this is the volatility implied by the options market. The price of an option depends on strike, tenor, vol, and others. If strike and tenor and others are fixed, you can derive the vol number directly from the option price.

From this point forward in this book, the term volatility in the various contexts will be abbreviated vol.

To explain a bit further, you can take the stock price history of Apple over the past decade to the present day and run a statistical analysis that will reveal its historical volatility. Past performance is no guarantee of future returns, so trading on historical volatility alone is like driving a car looking only through the rearview mirror. At the same time, however, historical volatility is valid information and useful as a basic guideline against which you can compare a forecast. If a forecast of actual vol is radically different from historical vol, it's important to pause and consider why that is and how it is justified.

Implied volatility, in contrast, is merely a price, a snapshot of market expectation of actual volatility at a particular moment. The day before an earnings report for a major corporation, the implied volatility reflects market expectation of volatility for the coming month. Low implied volatility may reflect market confidence that results will be in line with expectations. After the results are public, the implied volatility may be completely different. If results were much worse than expected, implied volatility will likely increase because of the "shock" of the results and the readjustment of expectations. Also if results were better than expected, implied volatility will again likely increase because of the surprise.

Actual volatility is what we are truly trying to determine, and forecasting models, although far from perfect, have become increasingly indispensible tools in trying to make sense from chaos. Just as investors forecast foreign exchange rates to capture superior carry, statistical methods have been developed over the past three decades to forecast actual volatility. Institutional investors have become more and more comfortable with the vol/variance investments partly because of the academic contribution in vol/variance research. Robert Engle won the Nobel prize in 2003 for his seminal work in volatility modeling and forecasting. It has educated a generation of "quants," myself included, who use the body of research to improve and apply forecasts of volatility to risk management and active investment.

Investing in Volatility Through Rules

Prior to the 2008 financial crisis, investment advice came down to building a diversified portfolio of stocks, bonds, currencies, notes, and other instruments. By spreading out the risk, even if one asset underperformed, the rest would compensate for the loss and produce a modest long-term gain. In the wake of the 2008 turmoil, achieving diversification has been challenging because "safe" assets, such as sovereign bonds, yield historically low returns. At the same time, "risky" assets, such as currencies, commodities, and credit, have become increasingly correlated, which has reduced the diversification. So you can either safely house funds in treasuries at near-zero returns, or if you invest in riskier assets, you risk another market crisis that could cause everything to crash together and at once.

Volatility is its own asset class, and just as in credit or equity markets, investors can expect to profit from taking risks in volatility premium, the difference between implied and realized volatility. An appealing characteristic of adding volatility investing to the portfolio is that it has low correlation with traditional asset classes, such as equity or bonds. Volatility, after all, exists independently of the market going up or down; it only matters that it's moving. After a major market crisis, volatility tends to be the best performing asset class. The recent history of the Lehman bankruptcy in 2008 and the Greek/European debt crises in 2010 has shown that immediately after the crises, while the economy is growing slowly, volatility outperforms. As discussed earlier in the case of flood insurance, it is right after the storm when insurance premiums are at their highest and the opportunity is greatest.

During market turmoil, however, all risky assets are highly correlated to the extreme. Strategies of receiving volatility premiums are no exception. That is why investing in the volatility premium through a disciplined rule based system is particularly important. The rules guide you whether to enter the trade or stay out, removing the temptation of investing on emotion and avoiding greed as well as fear. Without rules, the investor can be swept into the panic when the crisis event hits and likely will exit at a deep loss. Stung by the emotional and psychological toll of heavy losses, the typical reaction is to stand on the sidelines and lick your wounds, afraid of re-entering a turbulent market, when this is precisely the time you should be increasing your investment in the volatility premium.

The systematic rules introduced in this chapter employ simple statistics and market indicators. Statistics are by nature backward-looking because they are derived from historical data. Market indicators are derived from current market prices, which typically incorporate forward-looking components. The best results are achieved by combining both forward- and backward-looking approaches. Examples 1, 2, and 3 in this chapter provide a walk-through on how to construct simple yet effective rules in three markets: foreign exchange, equity indices, and rates.

After successfully constructing these three volatility strategies for three different markets, the next step is to build a volatility investment portfolio. This portfolio has an attractive risk-reward profile and low correlations with other risky asset classes, which is vital to diversification. What you actively work to establish is a benchmark of performance that fund managers or financial instruments involving volatility premium must outperform in order to justify fees imposed on investors.

Profiting from Volatility and Awareness of the Danger

For an investor, the first question to ask before investing in any strategy should always be, "Why will this strategy make money?" followed by, "And why hasn't the profit been traded away yet?" In the case of investing in the volatility premium, the strategy is profitable because the persistent return is a justified reward for bearing risk.

Playing the lottery, for example, exhibits a negative return in the long run. Even if you were to win $100 million, if the winnings were reinvested, you would eventually go broke. A dollar invested in the lottery is taxed by the government and pays the overhead of the lottery board, so despite the infrequent jackpot, returns are always negative. That is why the lottery is a horrible investment. If insurance were nationalized by the government and an exchange created in such a way that payouts precisely match premiums received, this would be an example of a return of zero. In the long run you neither make nor lose money. In the case of the volatility premium, just as is the case of a privatized insurance company, return is greater than zero because in the long term, you profit despite occasional market shocks.

You don't need to search very hard to see evidence of the persistent return of the volatility premium in the market. The risk premium is very real, and you need only look at the difference between the actual versus options market implied volatility of USDJPY one-month contracts. From January 2001 to July 2013, on the average, the market was paying 0.8% (or 0.8 volatility points) per day over what was actually realized. Out of more than 3,000 days, implied volatility was 67% of the time higher than realized volatility.

Realistically, it is hard to enter a volatility swap contract on a daily basis because, during market turmoil, volatility investments incur sharp losses. There would be liquidity constraints, higher bid/offer spread, and capital requirements. Over the long run, however, implied volatility is significantly higher than realized volatility for most markets, including stock and rates. Figures 1-2, 1-3, and 1-4 illustrate implied volatility versus actual volatility and the difference for FX, stock, and rates markets, to which we have applied investment rules. The discussion that follows demonstrates how rule based volatility strategies for these three markets are viable investments.

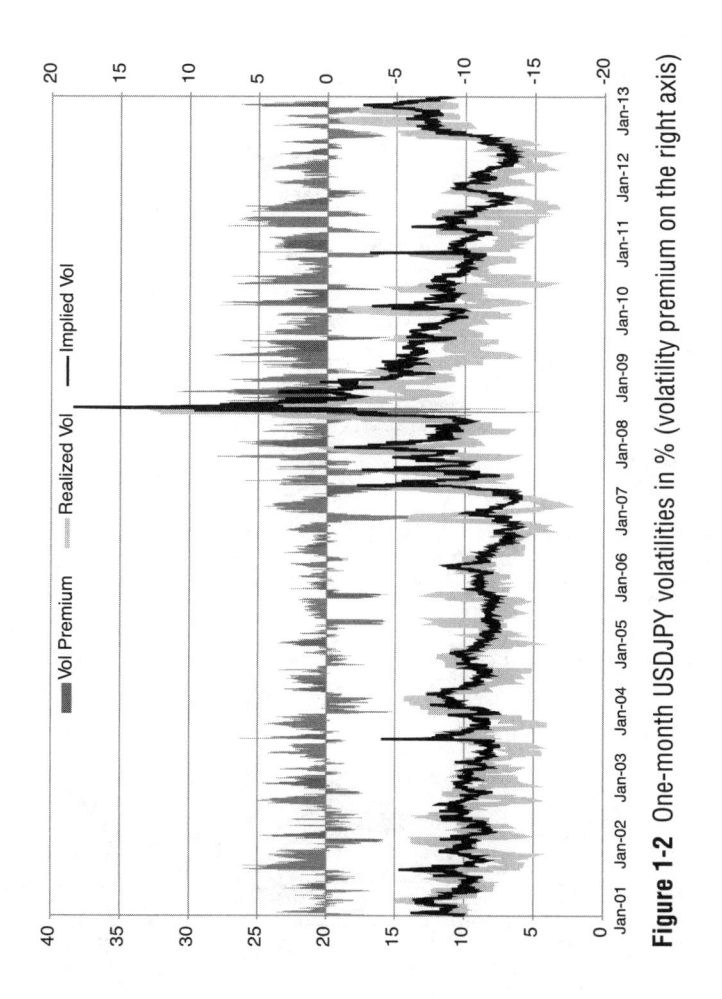

Figure 1-2 One-month USDJPY volatilities in % (volatility premium on the right axis)

22 Rule Based Investing

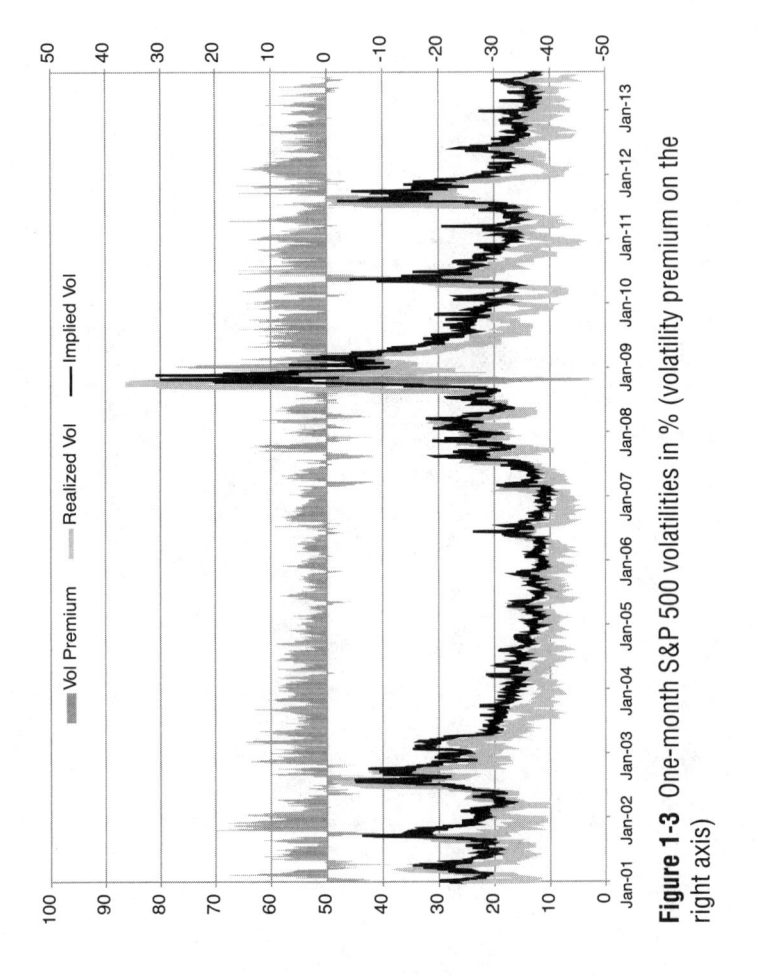

Figure 1-3 One-month S&P 500 volatilities in % (volatility premium on the right axis)

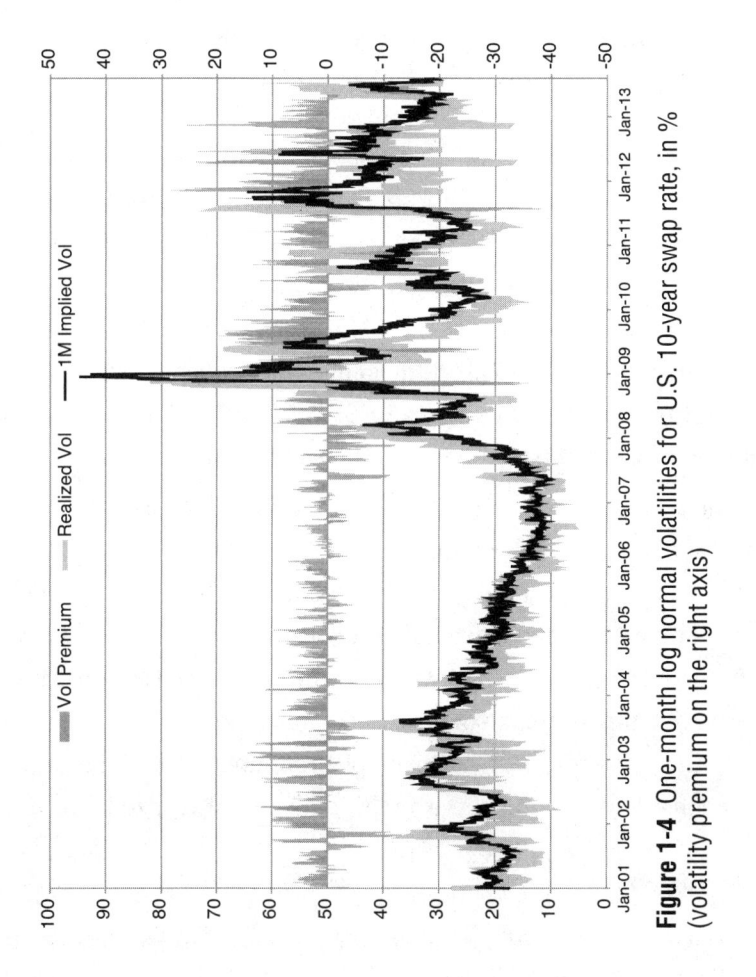

Figure 1-4 One-month log normal volatilities for U.S. 10-year swap rate, in % (volatility premium on the right axis)

In viewing these charts, realize that all the shaded area above the x- axis at the center of the graph represents profiting from the volatility premium. Only when there are the occasional dips below the x-axis is the volatility premium a losing investment. The overwhelming positive bias is a visual representation of what is meant by *persistent return*. The study by PIMCO's Rennison and Pedersen, covering 28 years of history for 14 volatility markets, including equities, commodities, currencies, and interest rates, showed strong evidence of volatility premium with magnitude ranging from 0.9% in currencies to 4.4% in commodity futures.[1] In particular, the study tested a monthly selling straddle strategy for these 14 markets and achieved annualized returns varying from 1.2% for currencies to 6.1% for commodity futures, with the Sharpe ratio ranging from 0.7 for currencies to 1.2 for U.S. rates and commodity futures.[2] The *Sharpe ratio* is a measure of the risk premium of an asset, meaning that between two assets with equal return, the one with a greater Sharpe required less risk to generate the same results and hence is the smarter investment.

The next question to ask is that if the volatility premium is real and exists, why hasn't the premium been traded away? After all, if we could buy apples for a dollar in France and sell them for ten dollars in Spain (assuming no tariffs and other restrictions), we would expect arbitrageurs to quickly exploit this price difference until it was erased. Why hasn't this occurred with the volatility premium? The reason is that the persistence of positive vol premiums, where the implied vol is consistently higher on average than actual realized vol, is not

---

[1] Rennison, Graham and Niels Pedersen, "The Volatility Risk Premium," PIMCO Viewpoint (September 2012).

[2] More precisely, according to Pimco's study, the average risk premium is 0.9%, 2.2%, 2.9%, and 4.4% for currencies, equity indices, 10-year interest rate swaptions, and commodity futures, respectively. Sharpe ratios are 0.7, 1.0, 1.2, and 1.2 for currencies, equity indices, 10-year interest rate swaptions, and commodity futures, respectively.

a market failure of mispricing; therefore, it cannot be argued that it should be traded away over time. The volatility premium will always exist because it is a natural by-product of a fundamental market force, which is an aversion to uncertainty.

The fear of uncertainty is as fundamental an economic principle as the time value of money. Economics undergraduates across the world are familiar with the question of whether a dollar today is worth as much as a dollar tomorrow. For multiple economic reasons, a dollar today is worth more. A dollar received today can be invested and generate interest overnight so that investment grows beyond a dollar. Also, there is the concern of inflation; a dollar tomorrow may have less buying power than a dollar today. What isn't discussed as often is the credit risk: Even if the dollar you received tomorrow was inflation-hedged and accrued the same interest as a dollar invested, despite these assurances, a dollar today is still worth more. The reason is uncertainty. All things being equal, a dollar today is guaranteed. A dollar tomorrow may seem likely and highly probable, but there could be a natural disaster, an accident, deceit, or some other catastrophe that foils our best-laid plans. The shrewd investor knows to expect the unexpected.

Volatility investors are compensated for providing protection against market turmoil in the same way that in fixed income there is a "term premium" for longer dated bonds to compensate for the uncertainty of future inflation and economic growth. What the volatility premium comes down to is receiving the "insurance premium" and paying back the actual realization, which in the long term is certain to be as naturally profitable a venture as selling insurance. If a disaster occurs, however, volatility spikes up, and the investment incurs losses.

The insurance company has a great business model in which it receives regular premiums that exceed the actual risk of losses. Nevertheless, losses will occur, and it will be painful when they do. Receiving implied volatility while paying actual volatility is like writing an option in which big losses are suffered when a crisis event occurs. In October of 2008, the simple strategy of receiving S&P 500 volatility premium lost more than 48% of the investment. Every investment that promises attractive returns carries a risk of significant losses, whether it is stock, bonds, currencies, or commodities. Or to put it another way, when rare events happen, long volatility premium suffers losses that are disproportionately large. Fortunately, however, the volatility premium strategies tend to recover quickly, more so than other asset classes, because it is precisely in the immediate aftermath of a crisis event when the volatility premium is richest. Insurance companies lose heavily when there are wildfires in the western United States that destroy hundreds of homes. However, they immediately started to recover those losses by the influx of new policy holders willing to pay the high premiums to protect them should they suffer the same fate as their neighbors. What it comes down to is that you want to invest in good risk and avoid the bad. Rule based investment strategies are how you will invest intelligently and avoid the bad risk brought on by emotion and greed.

The Examples of Rule Based Vol Investments

This section demonstrates simple rules to improve the performance of the naïve strategy of receiving volatility premium ("naïve" here means a simple "buy-and-hold" strategy) by using three examples from three markets: USDJPY from foreign exchange, S&P 500 from equity, and the U.S. 10-year swap rate from the interest rates market. Of the strategies developed, a common aspect of those rules applied to all volatility investment is to employ both statistical and market price implied indicators to dictate when *not* to invest in volatility premium. Statistical indicators involve information drawn from historical price data and hence are necessarily backward-looking. The universal disclaimer common to investment materials that "past performance is no guarantee of future return" is not entirely true because past performance does have inherent value. To completely ignore it discards relevant information. In contrast, market indicators are taken from real-time prices and are a snapshot of the market's expectation—and thus by nature are forward-looking indicators. By using these principles in conjunction, the final result is greater than the sum of its parts, as is shown in the following sections. Best of all is that by doing so you avoid the greed and reduce the sharp drawdown from major losses the occasional market crisis causes. When the rules indicate you should invest, especially immediately after a crisis, you follow the rules and not emotions, which might be to run and hide.

Example 1: Rule Based USDJPY Volatility Strategy

The task is to employ simple rules using common sense to outperform the naïve strategy that passively receives volatility premium. The naïve volatility strategy is defined as follows[3]: Every month, you invest the same amount of capital in USDJPY one-month volatility swap. The volatility swap obligates you at the end of the month to pay the realized volatility and receive a predetermined strike whose level is closely associated with one month at-the-money implied volatility. (An option is at-the-money if the strike price is the same as the current spot price.) In other words, the naïve strategy is to just "buy-and-hold" vol premium month after month, no matter what happens, like an automaton.

USDJPY is the first example for volatility investing because USDJPY is among the most liquid in Foreign Exchange (FX) markets, as are its derivatives. According to the Bank of International Settlement's survey,[4] the FX market has deep liquidity with a daily turnover

---

[3] You can also sell a one-month at-the-month straddle and delta hedge it every day to receive volatility premium.

[4] Bank for International Settlements, Triennial Central Bank Survey of Foreign Exchange and Derivatives Market Activity: 2001, 2004, 2007, and 2010.

of more than USD $4 trillion, and its options market a daily turnover of $200 billion. The FX volatility market is deep and diverse because of electic market participants with different objectives, such as hedging, reserve currency management, or investment. During the 2008 market turmoil, while other markets suffered from liquidity drying up, FX volatility market showed continued liquidity, albeit less so.

The persistence of USDJPY volatility premium is exhibited in the opening paragraph of this chapter and again in Figure 1-5: Over the period of 2001 to 2013, on average, one-month implied vol is 0.8% higher than actual vol for USDJPY volatility. Out of 150 months, 100 months implied vol was higher than actual realized vol, close to a 67% success rate. If you invest every month in the naïve strategy, assuming an average of 0.4 vol point transaction cost, the net return would be 4.75% per year, with a standard deviation of 10.1%, resulting in a Sharpe of 0.47, which is more than double that of buy-and-hold returns for the S&P 500 for the same period of time.

Something to mention here is the universal suggestion to fledgling investors that "buy-and-hold" is the strategy of choice; timing the market is impossible, so don't bother trying. "Timing the market" to capture the ups and avoid the lows is an incredibly difficult (if not impossible) skill, and the average investor does not have the foundation to even attempt "day trading" or trying to outsmart the market from home. Amateur investors trading frequently during the day are overwhelmingly funneling their funds to their brokers through transaction costs. By comparison, "buy-and-hold" is the better choice. The problem is that a completely passive strategy ignores the obvious in that there are times when clearly the market is nervous; spiking implied volatility rates are as visible a sign of market anxiety as when the hairs on a cat's back stand on end. These are periods to take risk off, and ignoring this information completely is as foolish as playing in traffic.

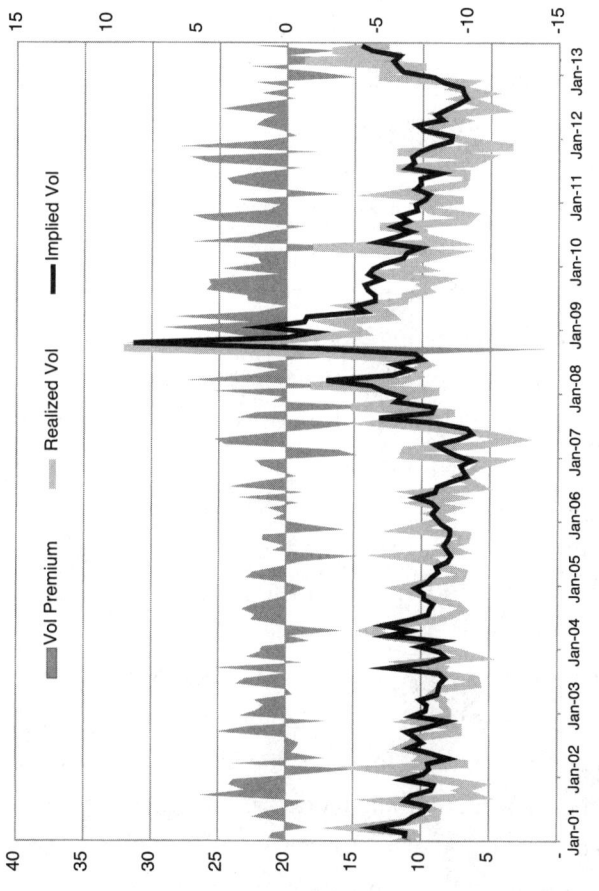

Figure 1-5 One-month USDJPY volatilities in %, monthly data (volatility premium on the right axis, after transaction cost)

As described previously, however, the naïve, long vol premium buy-and-hold strategy suffers large losses occasionally. For example, at the height of the financial crises in 2008, the naïve strategy would have suffered a loss of more than 14% in September. The key is to introduce simple indicators to alert yourself when turbulence threatens and avoid taking bad risk. There are endless ways of improving the naïve strategy. Especially when using the historical data available, it is tempting to impose rules that seem to maximize the historical performance. The danger here is getting lost in the alchemy of "data mining." *Data mining* involves pouring over historical prices to discover "gold" in the sense of a strategy that perfectly maximizes historical returns and hence should maximize future returns, however flawed this thinking. By imposing sufficient arbitrary rules and tweaking enough parameters, extraordinary returns are produced from historical data (granted these are theoretical profits). The flaw in this practice is that rules that produce magic returns from historical data seldom repeat their success with future price data. It is an easy trap to fall into. There is important information to be gained from historical prices, and simple rules based on broad patterns such as price volatility are helpful in creating a broad strategy, but as the rules become increasingly byzantine and specific in an effort to wring a perfect return from the historical data, the result is a "fool's gold" theory that fails in practice as new prices quickly display their own unique characteristics. Data mining exhibits diminishing returns the more elaborate the rules and patterns applied, and yet practitioners of these methods often blame their failing on their models not being complex enough. What we need are rules that make sense and are without too many parameters, so we avoid the temptation of data mining.

Two simple filters can be applied: The first filter is statistical and backward-looking, which uses USDJPY's own history to draw an intelligent inference about its future. The second is forward-looking and derived from the most recent, traded market prices that contain vital information about financial market sentiment.

Learning from History: GARCH Filter

A perfect forecast of upcoming actual volatility does not exist; otherwise this would be a very short book. A good statistical model can, however, help you build a sound forecast. By default many would use a rolling window standard deviation of daily returns as the forecast. Also popular is an exponential moving average of squared daily returns. These two proxies are easy to implement and are widely used by traders, analysts, and the like to get the first proxy of actual volatility. With the availability of intra-day data however, it is possible to just sum up high frequency return squares, which is itself a valid proxy for actual volatility (see, for example, Bollerslev and Andersen in the Bibliography). Figure 1-6 shows one-month historical volatility of USD-JPY from July 29 to August 13, 2013, computed using tick-by-tick data compared with using only one data point a day. The difference can often be substantial.

If high frequency data is not easy to obtain though, the next best thing you can do is use GARCH to measure and forecast actual volatility. *GARCH*[5] stands for Generalized Autoregressive Conditional Heteroskedasticity. As the name suggests, it is rather technical, and a detailed description can be found on various websites such as NYU's V-Lab.[6] Simply speaking, it says: Volatility is time varying, meaning it changes over time from times of calm to times of anxiety, and periods of different volatility tend to cluster together, which any good forecasting model should incorporate. GARCH is a simple, elegant statistical model that incorporates all these observed properties.

---

[5] Robert Engle first introduced models with time-varying volatility (ARCH) in his 1982 seminal paper "Autoregressive Heteroscedasticity with Estimate of the Variance of United Kingdom Inflation," *Econometrica* 50 (4), page 987-1008. Tim Bollerslev generalized it to GARCH in his 1986 paper, "Generalized Autoregressive Conditional Heteroskedasticity," *Journal of Econometrics*, pages 307-327.

[6] http://vlab.stern.nyu.edu.

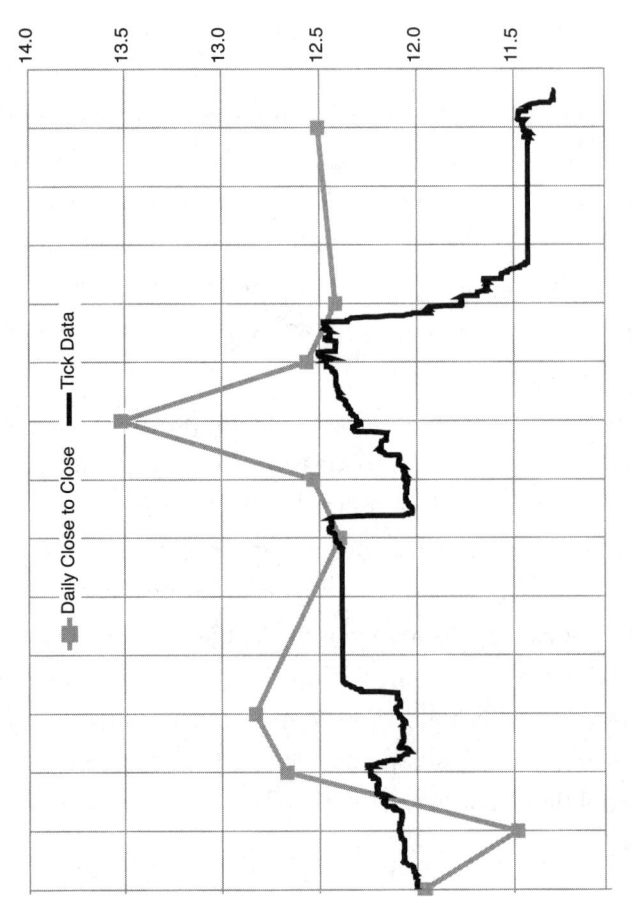

Figure 1-6 USDJPY one-month historical volatilities in % (daily close data versus tick-by-tick data)

Data Source: Bloomberg

Financial markets tend to behave anxiously in response to disruptive events such as wars, natural disasters, or market crises. During these crisis periods, volatility tends to be much higher than it typically is as prices sharply fluctuate. This means that the volatility of the financial markets is not constant over time. Times of calm are generally followed by calm; volatile days are followed by volatile days in a cluster. The term *heteroskedasticity* means a non-constant variance, such as that displayed by the markets, whereas *homoscedasticity* is a constant variance.

The assumption of constant variance is not valid to the behavior of financial markets.

As has been mentioned, the variance of stock prices during crisis times is very different than the variance of stock prices during times of calm. A more sophisticated model would have to reflect that behavior. Also, dependencies in the data would have to be taken into account. Clustering is observed because if today's stock price is extreme, it is likely tomorrow's price will be extreme as well. Also, these events display mean reversion, meaning that in weeks or months, an anxious market will eventually calm back down and return to its typical long-term behavior.

So GARCH in the end can be thought of as a simple yet sophisticated way to describe the volatility process. It is seen as sophisticated because, rather than weigh events from yesterday and events from last month equally, recent events are given greater weight through an exponentially weighted moving average. And the model also recognizes that financial markets display mean reversion. There are countless varieties of GARCH models, and for our purposes the simplest case of GARCH (1,1) will suffice. In GARCH (1,1), today's variance depends on yesterday's variance, the first "1", and yesterday's shock (in squares), the second "1".

Figure 1-7 shows GARCH (1,1)[7] predicted volatility against observed realized (measured using close-to-close returns), both with one-month tenor. As you can see, GARCH mimics the up and downs of realized vol well, with some lags due to its backward-looking characteristic. The model relies on historical data only, so necessarily market events must occur (and be read as data) before the model can respond.

Armed with a decent measure of actual volatility, the "sophisticated average" GARCH provides, you can now apply the first filter to the naïve vol premium strategy. Every month, you enter a volatility swap contract with one-month tenor in fixed amount of capital. The contract obligates you to receive a pre-determined strike level closely associated to the one-month at-the-money implied USDJPY volatility and pay upcoming realized volatility. If GARCH predicts upcoming high volatility, it indicates that recent market has experienced an unexpected large move. Something is happening behind the scenes that's raising anxiety. If GARCH predicts a higher move,[8] you don't take the risk of paying upcoming actual vol in the coming month. You stay on the sideline.

---

[7] GARCH(1,1) is the simplest model among the GARCH families. It uses only four parameters to describe the dynamics of return and its volatility.

[8] More specifically, if the difference between implied volatility and GARCH predicted actual volatility does not exceed a threshold, you will not take the risk of shorting volatility.

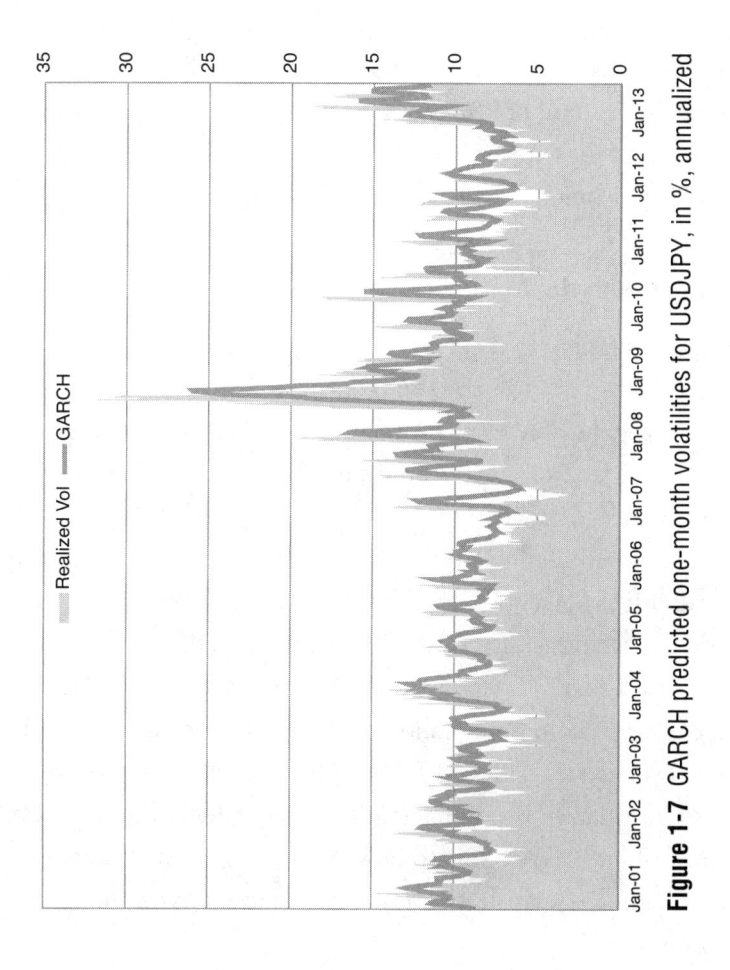

Figure 1-7 GARCH predicted one-month volatilities for USDJPY, in %, annualized

Table 1-1 compares the result of vol investing with and without the GARCH filter. From January 2001 to June 2013, imposing the GARCH filter would achieve a similar level of return as the naïve strategy, which is annualized 4.74%. Standard deviation, however, is reduced from 10.1% to 8%, hence the Sharpe ratio increases from 0.47 to 0.59. In particular, the largest one-month loss of 14.7%, which occurred in September 2008, is avoided by the GARCH filter. Out of 150 months from January 2001 to June 2013, the GARCH filter switched off a total of 40 months to avoid taking risk in USDJPY vol premium. All these results assume a 0.4% transaction cost (that is, you pay 0.4% per month), which is a conservative assumption.

Learning from the Market: VIX Filter

Short volatility to receive the vol premium is a strategy that tends to incur large losses during market turmoil. It is only natural, then, that you regularly read the VIX, the fear barometer, to access the market sentiment at any given time. The "VIX" is the ticker symbol for the Chicago Board Options Exchange Market Volatility Index, which is the implied volatility of S&P 500 index measured from put and call prices on at-the-money options. They are expressed as annual standard deviations of returns. It is a gauge of the market's expectation of stock market volatility over the next (average of) 30 days. For this reason it is commonly called the *fear index* because if the VIX is at a high level, it means the S&P 500 options market expects the next 30 days to be volatile. If options market prices reflect the opposite, that the S&P 500 will move smoothly, VIX will be low. In other words, VIX can be seen as a snapshot of a market's sentiment on the riskiness of the S&P 500.

Figure 1-8 shows how one-month USDJPY at-the-money implied volatility and VIX are highly correlated.

Table 1-1 Performance Statistics of USDJPY One-Month Volatility Premium Investment (Naïve Strategy vs. GARCH Filter, January 2001–June 2013)

	Average Annualized Return in %		Annualized Standard Deviation of Return in %		Maximal One Month Loss In %		Sharpe Ratio	
	Naïve	GARCH Filter	Naïve	GARCH Filter	Naïve	GARCH Filter	Naïve	GARCH Filter
2001	9.87	9.00	6.35	2.62	-1.67	0.18	1.55	3.43
2002	-4.52	-5.70	8.32	7.90	-4.48	-4.48	-0.54	-0.72
2003	10.97	8.39	5.00	3.87	-1.35	-1.35	2.20	2.17
2004	-1.00	2.99	5.73	5.12	-3.53	-3.53	-0.17	0.58
2005	-5.90	-1.26	6.62	5.68	-4.31	-4.31	-0.89	-0.22
2006	5.70	7.47	4.47	2.63	-1.41	-0.96	1.27	2.84
2007	-9.83	-8.07	11.45	10.63	-6.57	-6.57	-0.86	-0.76
2008	-2.61	6.06	21.63	10.49	-14.70	-7.63	-0.12	0.58
2009	33.04	30.84	7.47	8.01	-0.45	-0.03	4.42	3.85
2010	11.54	4.65	12.09	11.08	-8.28	-8.28	0.95	0.42
2011	18.84	13.84	9.52	9.57	-3.30	-3.30	1.98	1.45
2012–2013	-15.88	-18.10	9.24	9.17	-6.93	-6.93	-1.72	-1.97
Total	4.75	4.74	10.14	8.04	-14.70	-8.28	0.47	0.59

Source: Bloomberg

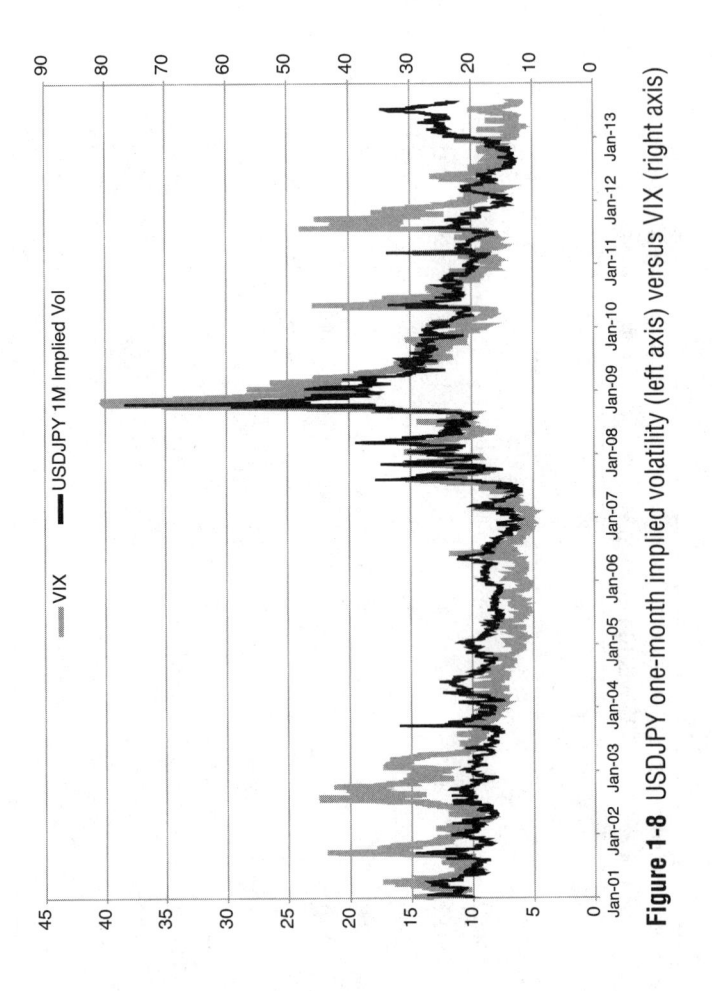

Figure 1-8 USDJPY one-month implied volatility (left axis) versus VIX (right axis)

The VIX filter, the second rule, is constructed in the following simple fashion: If yesterday's VIX closed higher than its own one-month average, you want to stay away from taking on risk in receiving vol premium. When the water is choppy, don't go out swimming. This simple yet intuitive filter helps us to boost average annual returns up from 4.75% to 5.64%; standard deviation is reduced from 10.1% to 6.9%. Although 2008 would have been one of the worst years for the naïve strategy with a 14.7% loss, the simple VIX filter would have nearly cut the loss in half down to 7.6%. Furthermore, Sharpe is increased from 0.47 to 0.82, indicating a superior return for the risk taken. Year to year performance breakdown is recorded in Table 1-2.

Are there other ways to construct a global risk indicator other than the VIX filter? The answer is yes. For example, the bid-ask spread is a good proxy for the liquidity of a market. Often market liquidity is directly linked to the magnitude of the bid-offer spread. If the bid-ask spread is larger than usual, this indicates market makers are nervous; willingness to provide liquidity has fallen. In this case, a simple rule based strategy should avoid any short vol (selling insurance) strategy from taking on risk. Another market barometer closely watched by professional investors is the TED Spread. The *TED Spread* is the difference between three-month LIBOR and T-bill rate. To elaborate, LIBOR is the overnight lending rate banks offer one another, and the T-bill rate is U.S. Treasury bill rate. Typically LIBOR rates and U.S. Treasuries should track closely together, with Treasuries seen as more secure at a lower rate. When LIBOR rates are just slightly above U.S. Treasuries, the spread is "tight," which means banks see loaning to each other as being almost as safe as U.S. Treasuries. When the spread widens, it indicates banks view lending to each other as less secure and more risky. High LIBOR rates and a high TED Spread often indicate problems in the banking system and global liquidity.

Table 1-2 Performance Statistics of USDJPY One-Month Volatility Premium Investment (Naïve Strategy vs. VIX Filter, January 2001–June 2013)

	Average Annualized Return in %		Annualized Standard Deviation of Return in %		Maximal One Month Loss In %		Sharpe Ratio	
	Naïve	*VIX Filter*	*Naïve*	*VIX Filter*	*Naïve*	*VIX Filter*	*Naïve*	*VIX Filter*
2001	9.87	8.08	6.35	3.67	-1.67	-0.79	1.55	2.20
2002	-4.52	0.32	8.32	7.39	-4.48	-4.48	-0.54	0.04
2003	10.97	6.00	5.00	3.98	-1.35	-1.35	2.20	1.51
2004	-1.00	0.82	5.73	3.36	-3.53	-1.72	-0.17	0.24
2005	-5.90	-4.56	6.62	6.41	-4.31	-4.31	-0.89	-0.71
2006	5.70	2.53	4.47	3.82	-1.41	-1.41	1.27	0.66
2007	-9.83	8.60	11.45	6.81	-6.57	-4.29	-0.86	1.26
2008	-2.61	7.20	21.63	14.47	-14.70	-7.63	-0.12	0.50
2009	33.04	19.54	7.47	7.07	-0.45	-0.45	4.42	2.76
2010	11.54	4.49	12.09	2.65	-8.28	0.02	0.95	1.69
2011	18.84	16.08	9.52	7.24	-3.30	-2.04	1.98	2.22
2012–2013	-15.88	-2.09	9.24	7.86	-6.93	-6.93	-1.72	-0.27
Total	4.75	5.64	10.14	6.86	-14.70	-7.63	0.47	0.82

Source: Bloomberg

Together and Stronger: Applying Both Filters

You can now apply both the GARCH and VIX filters to the naïve vol premium strategy for one-month USDJPY volatility. GARCH serves as a backward-looking filter, which utilizes the past information and tells you about the future average path of actual volatility. VIX is the most basic and widely available fear barometer, which reveals the anxiety level of the market. As recorded in Table 1-3, by applying both filters, the annualized return is 5.2% compared to the naïve strategy return of 4.8%; standard deviation is reduced closed to half from 10.1% to 5.9%, and a Sharpe ratio increases from 0.47 to 0.88. The rule based USDJPY vol strategy outperforms S&P 500 for the same period from 2001 to 2013, which accumulates an annualized return of 2.8% with a Sharpe ratio of 0.18. Using these simple rules, the results are nearly double the "buy-and-hold" return on the S&P during the same time period, with a better Sharpe (.9 rather than .18).

From January 2001 to June 2013, on a risk/reward basis, the rule based USDJPY volatility strategy outperformed benchmarks of holding passive risky assets such as MSCI world equity index (with a Sharpe of 0.16), and the results are on par with high-yield credit indices such as Barclays Capital's U.S. Corporate High Yield Index (Sharpe 0.85) and Global High Yield Index[9] (Sharpe 0.9). The performance comparison is summarized in Figure 1-9, illustrating cumulative returns with normalized volatility to an annualized 10% for all investments. The most desirable property of a rule based USDJPY volatility strategy is that it is not correlated with these risky assets. The correlations of monthly returns between USDJPY volatility strategy and S&P 500, MSCI World Equity, U.S. High Yield, and Global High Yield index are -0.10, 0.08, 0.01 and 0.01, respectively.

---

[9] Barclays Capital Global High Yield Index in USD, return unhedged. For a list of Barclay's indices, see https://indices.barcap.com/index.dxml.

Table 1-3 Performance Statistics of USDJPY One-Month Volatility Premium Investment (Naïve Strategy vs. Joint Filter, January 2001–June 2013)

	Average Annualized Return in %		Annualized Standard Deviation of Return in %		Maximal One Month Loss In %		Sharpe Ratio	
	Naïve	Joint Filter	Naïve	Joint Filter	Naïve	Joint Filter	Naïve	Joint Filter
2001	9.87	7.46	6.35	2.36	-1.67	0.18	1.55	3.17
2002	-4.52	0.32	8.32	7.39	-4.48	-4.48	-0.54	0.04
2003	10.97	6.90	5.00	3.75	-1.35	-1.35	2.20	1.84
2004	-1.00	3.08	5.73	2.67	-3.53	-0.79	-0.17	1.15
2005	-5.90	-0.52	6.62	5.32	-4.31	-4.31	-0.89	-0.10
2006	5.70	4.30	4.47	1.59	-1.41	-0.96	1.27	2.71
2007	-9.83	6.62	11.45	6.31	-6.57	-4.29	-0.86	1.05
2008	-2.61	4.24	21.63	10.36	-14.70	-7.63	-0.12	0.41
2009	33.04	17.34	7.47	7.27	-0.45	0.02	4.42	2.38
2010	11.54	2.77	12.09	2.50	-8.28	0.02	0.95	1.11
2011	18.84	13.43	9.52	7.20	-3.30	-2.04	1.98	1.87
2012–2013	-15.88	-3.19	9.24	7.84	-6.93	-6.93	-1.72	-0.41
Total	4.75	5.21	10.14	5.91	-14.70	-7.63	0.47	0.88

Source: Bloomberg

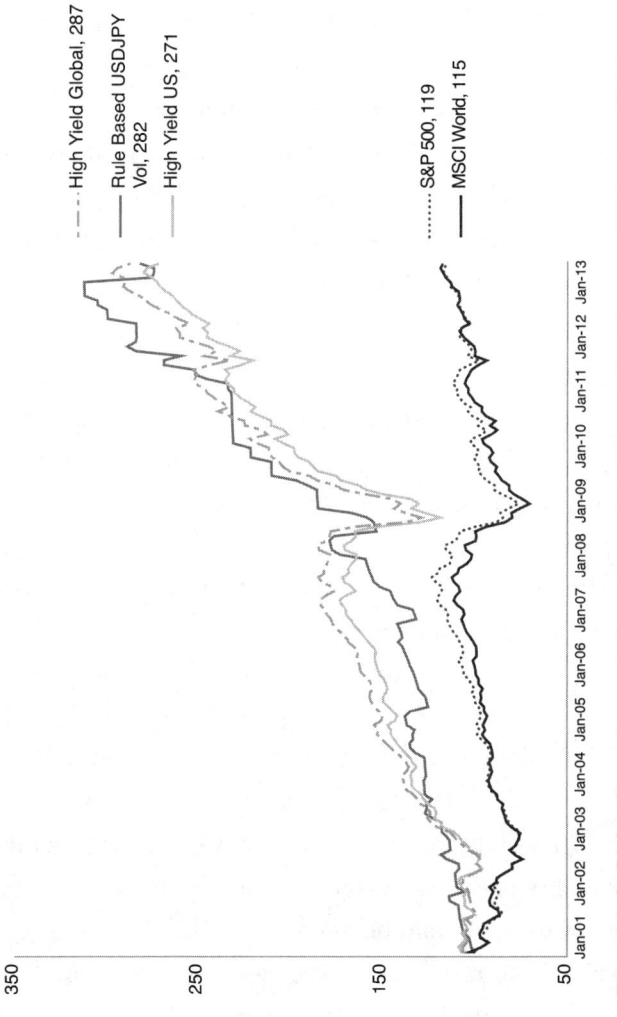

Figure 1-9 Risk-adjusted cumulative returns (volatility = 10%), January 2001–June 2013

Example 2: S&P 500 Volatility

The next example is investing in S&P 500 volatility. To invest in foreign exchange volatility, a volatility swap is the simplest instrument; in the equity markets volatility premium is best captured through a variance swap. Investing in volatility is also possible through selling a one-month at-the-money options straddle and delta hedge until the maturity (short straddle is an option strategy that pays out if prices remain within a certain range, meaning low volatility is expected). Futures on the VIX have become more liquid, and recently ETFs have been created and traded that enable individual investors to access the equity index volatility market. There are more selections and accessibility to the volatility market now than there have ever been.

There exists a natural excess of market participants interested in buying protection, such as pensions and 401ks. Pension funds and 401ks are market behemoths that desire safe and steady returns and will pay for market "insurance" to protect from volatility. As mentioned before, there is a greater number of natural insurance buyers than insurance sellers. This imbalance of high demand and low supply is the driving force behind the persistence of S&P 500 vol premium: Over the period of January 2001–June 2013, on the average, implied vol was 3.7 vol points (about 21%) higher than actual vol for one-month at-the-money volatility. Out of 150 months, for 122 months implied vol was higher than actual realized vol, a success rate of 81%. If you invest every month in a naïve strategy of just receiving and holding volatility premium, assuming you pay an average of 1.5% to do so, the net return would be an annualized 25.7%, with a standard deviation of 26%, a resulting Sharpe close to 1, compared with 0.18 for S&P 500 index itself for the same period of time. Yes that is correct, playing the role of the insurance company and collecting the vol premium for the S&P 500, with a naïve buy-and-hold strategy produced returns of 25.7%. Figure 1-10 illustrates the persistence of positive vol returns:

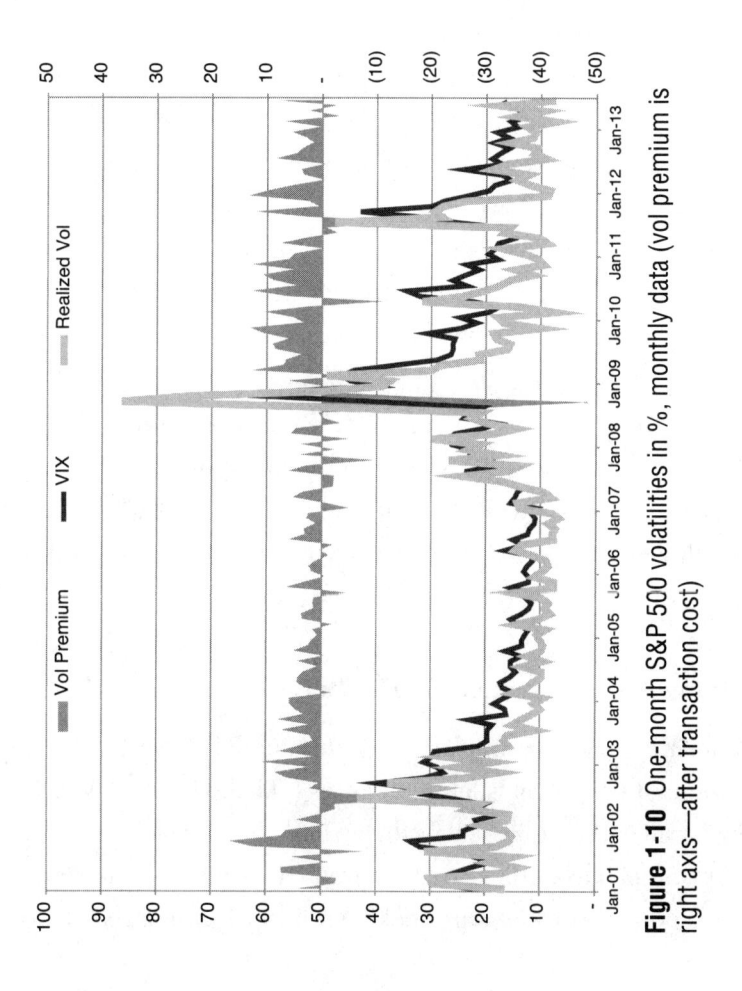

Figure 1-10 One-month S&P 500 volatilities in %, monthly data (vol premium is right axis—after transaction cost)

With this astonishing performance, why improve the simple strategy? The angst of all investors is the large negative skewed tail risk, meaning when extreme events occur, the effect is catastrophic. In 2008, the naïve vol strategy of just receiving vol premium and holding blindly, would have lost the investor close to 85%, nearly all of the capital. No institutional investors would have survived this kind of loss without asset under management fleeing away. In 2009 however, the naïve strategy swung back into profitability and returned 82%. So for those investors who suffered the loss in 2008 and subsequently were scared out of the market and stood by the sidelines of vol investing, they would not have had a chance to recover and profit from the rebound of the 2009 market environment. That is why rules are essential, particularly with volatility, which is an emotionally charged market capable of producing great gains and great losses.

Using the two simple filters, the next rules introduced in this chapter aim to "smooth out" the big swings of volatility investing and reduce the impact of crisis events. Again, these filters won't magically eliminate losses but will soften the blow. By reducing the negative skew, the rule based volatility strategy is likely to survive in the long run and thus produce profit from long-term gains.

Learning from History: GARCH Filter

Again, using the simplest statistical model, GARCH (1,1), you can forecast the actual volatility. Figure 1-11 shows the GARCH predicted realized volatility versus the actual realized volatility. It mimics the up and downs of the actual realized vol rather well, however with some lag due to its backward-looking reliance on statistical data.

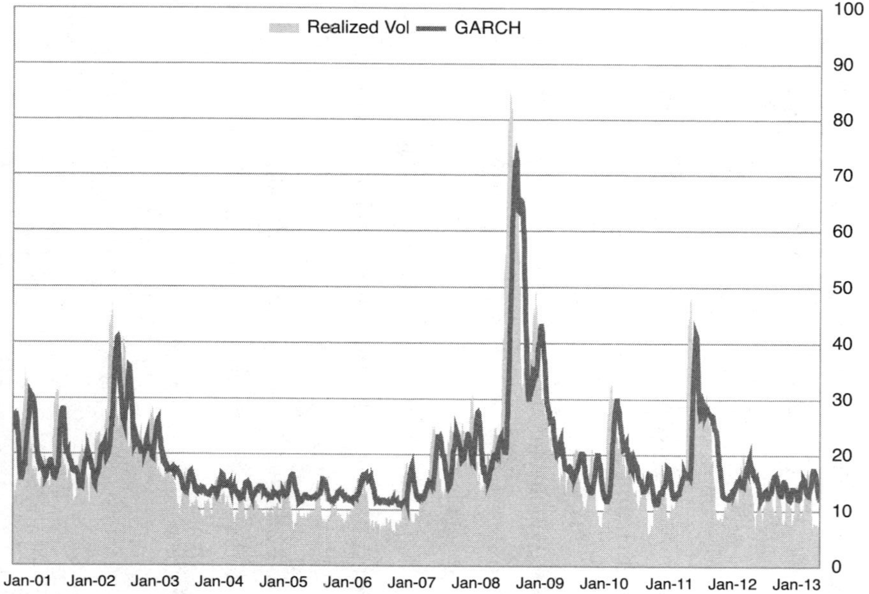

Figure 1-11 GARCH predicted one-month volatilities for S&P 500 Index, in %, annualized

The GARCH strategy works as it did before: Every month you invest the same amount of capital to receive volatility premium,[10] by entering a trade to receive a predetermined strike closely related to at-the-money implied volatility or variance and to pay upcoming realized volatility or variance. The GARCH filter is applied in the following way: If GARCH's forecast of conditional variance is high because the most recent market data shows an exceptional movement (tremors of volatility if you will), you do not take the risk of going short vol in the coming month. The rule would tell us that this is a "risk off" month. Table 1-4 records the effect of applying the GARCH filter. From January 2001 to June 2013, the GARCH filter improved performance from an annualized return of 25.7% to 28.6%, and annualized standard deviation reduced dramatically from 25.9% to 14.3%. Sharpe ratio is increased from 0.99 to 2.6. The dramatic improved Sharpe indicates you are taking much more intelligent risk. It is, after all, intelligent to stay indoors if the weather forecast threatens a coming storm. All results are net of a transaction cost of 1.5% per trade.

Most significantly, in 2008, the GARCH filter helped to turn the large loss that resulted from the naïve strategy into profit. Figure 1-12 displays the GARCH signal in 2008 together with the S&P 500's volatility premium. For the months of August through December 2008, GARCH signaled risk-off from the volatility market, hence avoiding a loss of more than 90%.

---

[10] Although in equity market variance swap is much more commonly traded than volatility swap, the term volatility is used for the purpose of consistency.

Table 1-4 Performance Statistics of S&P 500 One-Month Volatility Premium Investment (Naïve Strategy vs. GARCH Filter, January 2001–June 2013)

	Average Annualized Return in %		Annualized Standard Deviation of Return in %		Maximal One Month Loss In %		Sharpe Ratio	
	Naïve	GARCH Filter	Naïve	GARCH Filter	Naïve	GARCH Filter	Naïve	GARCH Filter
2001	52.13	3.70	23.82	0.36	-7.57	0.16	2.19	10.22
2002	-5.25	3.85	24.26	2.05	-19.35	0.12	-0.22	1.87
2003	58.07	47.25	10.63	9.30	1.12	0.11	5.46	5.08
2004	32.53	28.38	8.01	8.19	-1.79	-1.79	4.06	3.47
2005	16.53	12.74	9.62	4.29	-4.39	-0.54	1.72	2.97
2006	20.62	15.34	7.27	4.49	-1.96	-1.21	2.84	3.41
2007	-1.81	3.93	15.95	15.64	-9.66	-9.66	-0.11	0.25
2008	-84.31	7.26	58.00	10.32	-48.45	-4.72	-1.45	0.70
2009	81.61	52.60	16.15	16.78	-4.27	-4.27	5.05	3.14
2010	74.00	57.26	22.10	15.81	-11.05	0.02	3.35	3.62
2011	18.85	13.97	32.58	32.39	-23.93	-23.93	0.58	0.43
2012-2013	35.18	23.92	13.66	12.91	-3.14	-3.14	2.57	1.85
Total	25.75	23.15	25.94	14.30	-48.45	-23.93	0.99	1.62

Source: Bloomberg

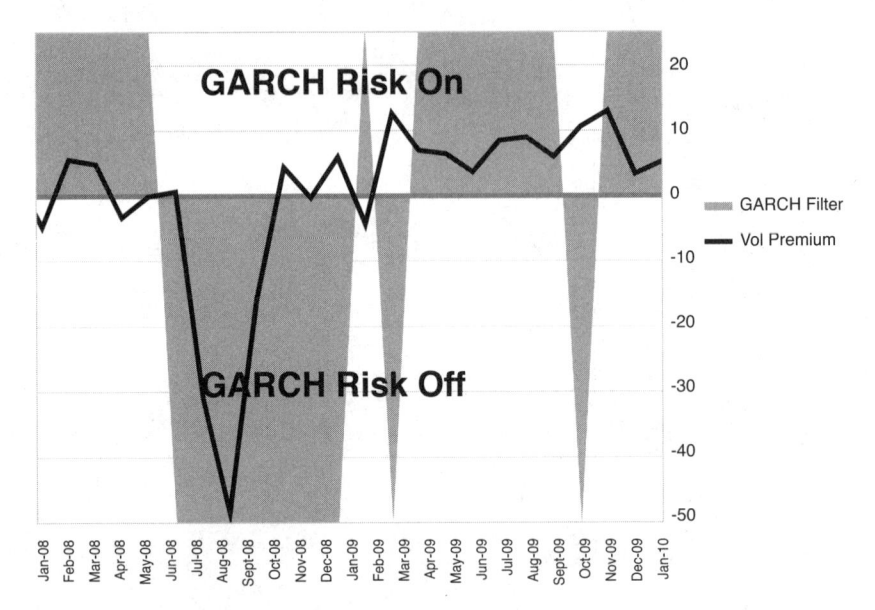

Figure 1-12 GARCH Risk On/Off for S&P 500 Volatility Investing

Learning from the Market: VIX Filter

For S&P 500 volatility, VIX itself is the obvious choice for constructing a market implied, forward-looking risk on/off filter. In the same fashion as for USDJPY volatility premium, each month, we only invest in S&P 500 volatility premium if yesterday's VIX closes below its own historical average.

The resulting benefits of applying a VIX filter are demonstrated in Table 1-5 and Figure 1-13. Overall returns increase from 25.7% to 28.0%, standard deviation reduced from 25.9% to 16.7%. What to look at in the filter is that in 2008 it helped to reduce maximal monthly loss from 48% to zero so that 2008 overall performance transformed from a large loss of -84% to -27%. By applying this simple VIX filter, investing in vol premium has reached a Sharpe ratio as high as 1.6, net of transaction cost of 1.5% per month.

Table 1-5 Performance Statistics of S&P 500 One-Month Volatility Premium Investment (Naïve Strategy vs. VIX Filter, January 2001–June 2013)

	Average Annualized Return in %		Annualized Standard Deviation of Return in %		Maximal One Month Loss In %		Sharpe Ratio	
	Naïve	*VIX Filter*	*Naïve*	*VIX Filter*	*Naïve*	*VIX Filter*	*Naïve*	*VIX Filter*
2001	52.13	3.70	23.82	0.36	-7.57	0.16	2.19	10.22
2002	-5.25	18.24	24.26	9.75	-19.35	0.15	-0.22	1.87
2003	58.07	58.07	10.63	10.63	1.12	1.12	5.46	5.46
2004	32.53	32.53	8.01	8.01	-1.79	-1.79	4.06	4.06
2005	16.53	16.53	9.62	9.62	-4.39	-4.39	1.72	1.72
2006	20.62	20.71	7.27	7.25	-1.96	-1.96	2.84	2.86
2007	-1.81	-1.51	15.95	14.35	-9.66	-9.66	-0.11	-0.11
2008	-84.31	-23.04	58.00	33.40	-48.45	-30.97	-1.45	-0.69
2009	81.61	81.61	16.15	16.15	-4.27	-4.27	5.05	5.05
2010	74.00	61.35	22.10	21.65	-11.05	-11.05	3.35	2.83
2011	18.85	28.72	32.58	15.23	-23.93	-2.72	0.58	1.89
2012-2013	35.18	32.43	13.66	13.87	-3.14	-3.14	2.57	2.34
Total	25.75	28.03	25.94	16.76	-48.45	-30.97	0.99	1.67

Source: Bloomberg

Together and Stronger: Applying Both Filters

What happens when you combine both GARCH and VIX filters to the naïve strategy? The results are illustrated in Table 1-6. Applying both filters, an annualized return of 23.4% is realized, with a standard deviation of 11.9% and a doubled Sharpe ratio from 1 to 2.

Although the USDJPY volatility strategy from the previous example exhibits little correlation with the risky benchmarks, the rule based S&P 500 volatility strategy has a higher correlation with the index as well as other risky benchmarks. For the period January 2001–June 2013, the correlations with S&P 500, MSCI World Equity Index, U.S. High Yield, and Global High Yield Index are 0.32, 0.29, 0.25, and 0.24, respectively.

With GARCH outperforming in 2008 the VIX filter in the example of S&P 500 volatility investing, it is tempting to apply the backward-looking filter GARCH alone and discard VIX filter rule or any forward-looking type indicator. An important thing to remember is that the VIX filter rule shown here is the simplest form of moving average, comparing the current level of the VIX to its mean over a window of time, and as a result there is great room for improvement. To understand why the joint filter produced a slightly lower return, understand that the joint filter switched risk "off" for some borderline volatile months. Had risk stayed on, it would have turned out those months were actually profitable and hence the higher return achieved by applying GARCH filter alone. What is important to note, however, is that keeping risk on during those months, although profitable, was not a smart risk to take. The joint filter has the highest Sharpe, indicating more intelligent risk. Further, there are other indicators than the VIX alone; some suggested by academic research are to use the variance swap term structure or the shape of the variance curve.[11] The next example explicitly applies the shape of the vol curve to volatilities of U.S. swap rates market.

---

[11] Examples are Egloff, Daniel, Markus Leippold, and Liuren Wu, "The Term Structure of Variance Swap Rates and Optimal Variance Swap Investments," *Journal of Financial and Quantitative Analysis*, 45(5) (October 2010): 1279–1310, and Bernales, Alejandro and Guidolin Massimo, "Can We Forecast the Implied Volatility Surface Dynamics of Equity Options? Predictability and Economic Value Tests," Working Papers 456, IGIER (Innocenzo Gasparini Institute for Economic Research), Bocconi University, 2012.

Table 1-6 Performance Statistics of S&P 500 One-Month Volatility Premium Investment (Naïve Strategy vs. Joint Filter, January 2001–June 2013)

	Average Annualized Return in %		Annualized Standard Deviation of Return in %		Maximal One Month Loss In %		Sharpe Ratio	
	Naïve	Joint Filter	Naïve	Joint Filter	Naïve	Joint Filter	Naïve	Joint Filter
2001	52.13	3.70	23.82	0.36	-7.57	0.16	2.19	10.22
2002	-5.25	3.85	24.26	2.05	-19.35	0.12	-0.22	1.87
2003	58.07	47.25	10.63	9.30	1.12	0.11	5.46	5.08
2004	32.53	28.38	8.01	8.19	-1.79	-1.79	4.06	3.47
2005	16.53	12.74	9.62	4.29	-4.39	-0.54	1.72	2.97
2006	20.62	15.34	7.27	4.49	-1.96	-1.21	2.84	3.41
2007	-1.81	0.94	15.95	14.21	-9.66	-9.66	-0.11	0.07
2008	-84.31	3.80	58.00	9.74	-48.45	-4.72	-1.45	0.39
2009	81.61	52.60	16.15	16.78	-4.27	-4.27	5.05	3.14
2010	74.00	57.26	22.10	15.81	-11.05	0.02	3.35	3.62
2011	18.85	23.85	32.58	15.10	-23.93	-2.72	0.58	1.58
2012-2013	35.18	23.92	13.66	12.91	-3.14	-3.14	2.57	1.85
Total	25.75	23.42	25.94	11.87	-48.45	-9.66	0.99	1.97

Source: Bloomberg

54 RULE BASED INVESTING

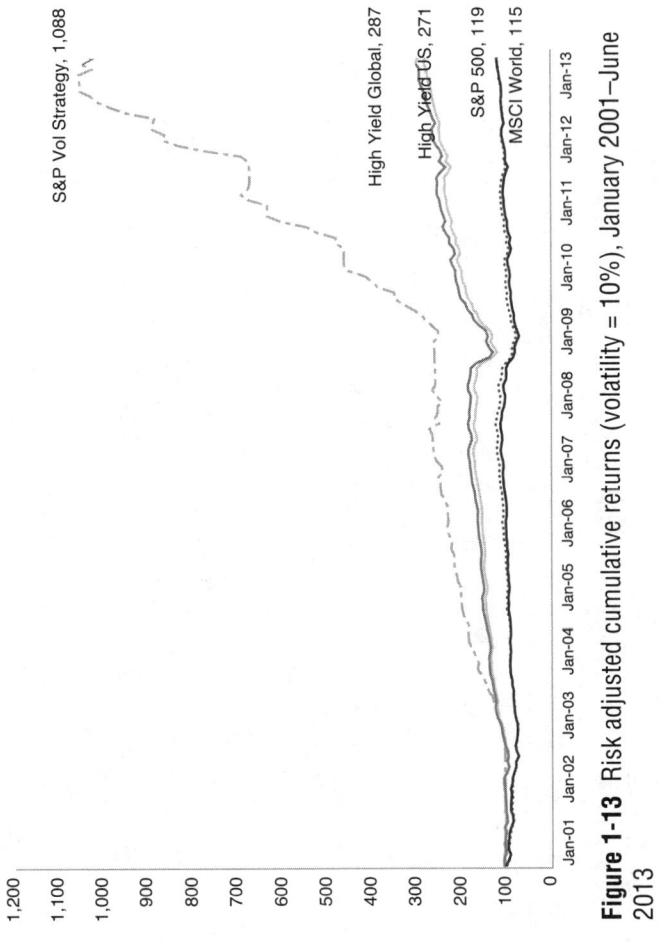

Figure 1-13 Risk adjusted cumulative returns (volatility = 10%), January 2001–June 2013

Example 3: Swap Rates Volatility

This third and final example demonstrates how to create and apply simple rules to aid you in avoiding major losses in volatility premium investments in interest rate markets, with a focus on studying the volatility premium for 10-year U.S. swap rates. The persistent alpha of the volatility premium is particularly pronounced in the U.S. swap rates market where mortgage hedging against prepayment risk creates a natural demand for shorter dated volatility. Consider that from January 2001 to June 2013, the implied volatility for one-month at-the-money swaption exceeded the realized volatility 67% of the time. The average difference was 1.8%. As Figure 1-14 shows, however, during periods of market turmoil, volatility investments experience sudden heavy losses. This is the problem that plagues the "naïve" strategy of simply buying and holding vol premium. When a market crisis occurs, receiving the volatility premium (short vol) has a major downside. In the business of earthquake insurance, it is an expectation that suddenly massive payouts will occur when an earthquake occurs because it affects a wide area.

The rules introduced here, though simple, are designed to help you escape or at least dodge the full impact of a market crisis event. The aim of the rule based investment strategy introduced in the following section is to use both backward-looking statistical models as well as forward-looking market indicators to avoid shorting volatilities when turbulence threatens. Whether you stay in the trade or exit the position, it is no longer determined by emotion or personal market views, but by rules that act as on/off switches for whether we do or do not receive the volatility premium for a particular month.

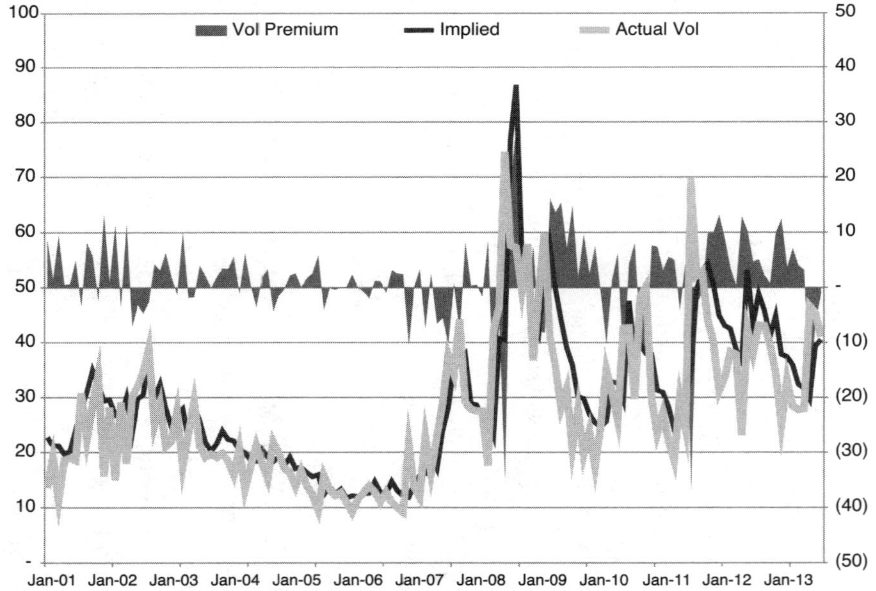

Figure 1-14 One-month U.S. 10-year swap rate volatilities in %, monthly data (vol premium is right axis—after transaction cost)

Interest rate vol or variance swap is much less liquid than Foreign Exchange or equity markets. The simplest way to capture vol premium in swap rates is to sell an at-the-money swaption straddle and delta hedge it until expiration.[12] One-month at-the-money straddle is very liquid, which is ideal. Liquidity itself is a function of the risk premium a market is charging. When a market maker trades with a client, the market maker is temporarily exposed to the risk of the other side of the client's trade. To clear that position and cancel out the risk, they must trade away the risk to someone else. The compensation the market maker asks for shouldering the inherent risk of this service is the bid/ask spread. The bid/ask spread guarantees the transaction is biased in favor of the market maker. When a market has many participants, it is easy to get in and out of trades, the risk of market making is minimal, and the supply/demand of participants quickly establishes a narrow range of prices, which all together means liquidity is good. When liquidity is bad there is uncertainty on what the correct price is, the bid/ask spread reflects this risk meaning expensive transactions, and even if you want to exit your position, you might be stuck because there's no counterparty. You typically want to invest in liquid markets because the transaction cost will be minimal (meaning a tight bid/ask spread), and you are able to quickly exit a position if you need to—at minimal expense.

Along the same lines as the two previous volatility strategies, you can now apply two filters: the first one is statistical and looks backward, that is, learning from the historical movement of the swap rate itself to draw some inference about its future. The second is a forward-looking indicator derived from traded market prices.

---

[12] For details of interest rates swaption please see, for example, Tuckman, Bruce and Angle Serrat. *Fixed Income Securities Tools for Today's Markets* 3rd ed. Wiley Finance, 2011.

Learning from History: GARCH Filter

Again, using the simplest statistical model, GARCH (1,1), you can forecast actual volatility. As previously noted, GARCH (1,1) has the advantage of being easy to estimate, and it models volatility with many desirable properties such as time varying volatility and persistence. Figure 1-15 shows the GARCH predicted volatility compared to the realized volatility. As you can see, GARCH mimics the ups and downs of realized vol rather well; however, there is some lag due to its backward-looking characteristics. A statistical model necessarily implies market events must first occur and be entered as data before the model can react, hence a persistent lag.

This GARCH strategy works as it has before: To receive the vol premium, every month you sell the same amount of one-month straddle and delta hedge. If GARCH predicts a high volatility in the near future, so that vol premium does not exceed an economic threshold, you do not want to take the risk of short volatility in the coming month. If yesterday's return has an above average amount of movement (that is, the return square is high), this information will reveal in a higher GARCH reading. Then you don't want to go short volatility because it is likely to be high in the coming months. Again GARCH here serves as a "sophisticated average" of return movement.

CHAPTER 1 • RULE BASED VOLATILITY INVESTMENT   59

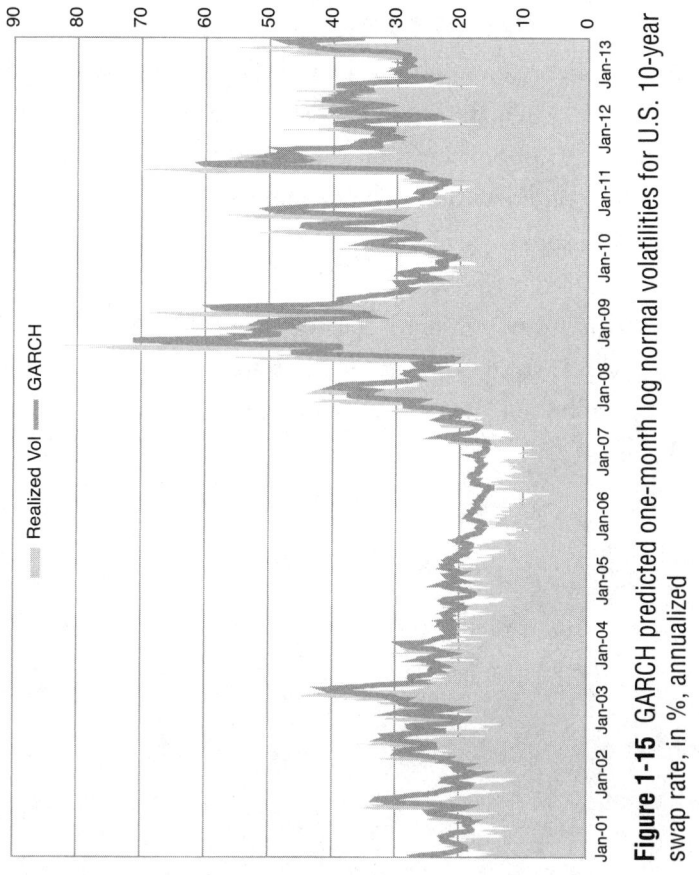

Figure 1-15 GARCH predicted one-month log normal volatilities for U.S. 10-year swap rate, in %, annualized

Table 1-7 records the effect of applying the GARCH filter. From January 2001 to June 2013, compared with simple short straddle strategy, the GARCH filter achieved a slightly lower annualized return from 18.1% to 17.4%. The standard deviation of the returns however, was improved from 28% to 21%. The GARCH filter worked very well in 2011's second European debt crises by reducing the maximum one-month loss of 37% to 4% and improved the year's return by almost three-fold. GARCH, however, is not the "Holy Grail." It has its limitations in the U.S. swaptions market. The reason for the slightly lower return is when the trade is "risk off," you avoid both ends of your return distribution both on the negative end of losses as well as the positive end of profits. The overall risk profile is superior, and the return just slightly less, making for a smarter investment, but still the slight loss in returns shows the limitation of a very simple model–there is enormous potential for improvement. Figure 1-16 illustrates that the GARCH strategy failed to filter out the large loss experienced in October 2008 and missed out the market rebound immediately after the crises.

Table 1-7 Performance Statistics of U.S. 10-Year Swap Rate One-Month Volatility Premium Investment (Naïve Strategy vs. GARCH Filter, January 2001–June 2013)

	Average Annualized Return in %		Annualized Standard Deviation of Return in %		Maximal One Month Loss In %		Sharpe Ratio	
	Naïve	GARCH Filter	Naïve	GARCH Filter	Naïve	GARCH Filter	Naïve	GARCH Filter
2001	11.01	9.61	17.96	10.84	-11.47	-5.33	0.61	0.89
2002	47.41	53.40	17.69	15.49	-3.37	0.14	2.68	3.45
2003	16.19	11.63	21.11	15.53	-7.10	-4.73	0.77	0.75
2004	31.94	26.94	12.13	12.52	-1.78	-1.78	2.63	2.15
2005	5.65	9.50	8.53	3.41	-4.19	0.07	0.66	2.79
2006	3.68	5.89	8.24	7.81	-4.05	-4.05	0.45	0.75
2007	-27.08	-15.28	18.64	14.28	-10.35	-10.35	-1.45	-1.07
2008	-5.03	-37.73	57.39	41.91	-34.65	-34.65	-0.09	-0.90
2009	73.71	68.29	29.92	26.24	-8.19	-7.80	2.46	2.60
2010	-8.94	9.54	28.90	22.81	-13.63	-12.66	-0.31	0.42
2011	14.29	41.82	45.04	18.01	-36.59	-4.01	0.32	2.32
2012-2013	26.38	11.41	24.65	25.45	-17.55	-17.55	1.07	0.45
Total	18.13	17.40	27.88	21.12	-36.59	-34.65	0.65	0.82

Source: Bloomberg

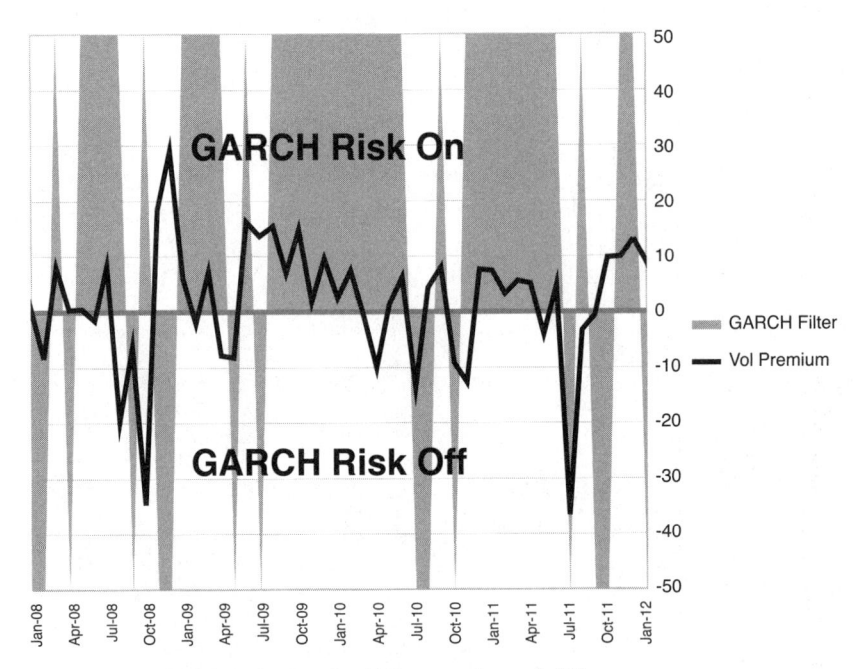

Figure 1-16 GARCH filtering for U.S. swaption volatility

Learning from the Market: (Slope of) Vol Curve Filter

The next filter is constructed by using the implied volatility curve as an on/off switch for the naïve strategy of selling one-month straddles. You will see how the volatility curve itself has the filtering power to root out potential market crises. Under normal market conditions, the volatility curve should be upward slopping, that is, the price of longer dated options should be higher than shorter dated options because more uncertainty is priced in. When the options market expects an eminent crisis, the prices for short maturity options spike up even more than the prices for longer dated options. This is strange as the market is saying that tomorrow is much more uncertain than a year from now. This leads to an inverted vol curve. Figure 1-17 shows the different shapes of log normal vol curve corresponding to different market sentiments: During normal market conditions, vol curve is upward sloping or flat. However, for example, during 2008 Global Financial Crisis, the vol curve was particularly inverted; that is, one-month at-the-money vol was much higher that the longer dated vol. The inverted vol curves could be observed in almost all option markets during that time.

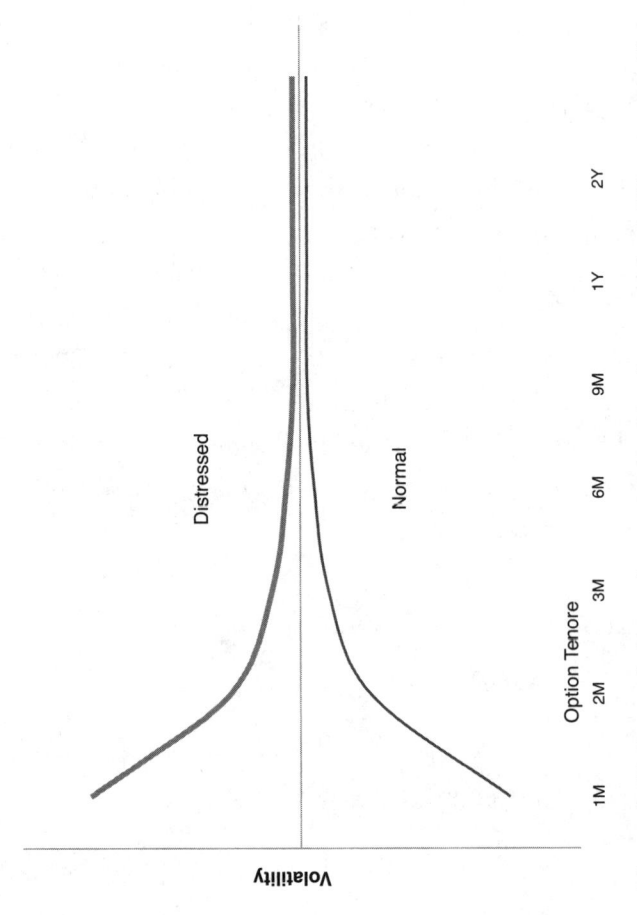

Figure 1-17 Upward versus downward slopping log normal volatility curve, in %

You can apply the vol curve filter in the following manner: Focus on only two points along the vol curve, the one-month versus the one-year option maturities. These are simple basic rules and parameters derived from experience rather than data mining–you can capture the bulk of the market information without fooling yourself with an excess of conditions. Define the slope as the difference (in ratio) between at-the-money volatilities of one-month and one-year options for U.S. 10-year swap rates and only invest in the volatility premium (that is, selling straddle to receive the vol premium if yesterday's vol curve slope is *not* higher than its own historical average. In other words, if the short end of the vol curve is high compared with the long end of the vol curve (meaning the near future is uncertain), you do not want to take the risk of investing in vol premium because it implicitly implies that the options market is pricing an imminent crisis. The options market can be right or wrong. We won't know until the month is over. As a cautious investor, however, you do not want to take the uneducated risk of betting against the option markets under such extraordinary circumstances.

The resulting benefit of applying a volatility curve filter is demonstrated in the Table 1-8 and Figure 1-18. Overall return is lower than that of naïve and GARCH strategy, but risk profile is better. Standard deviation is reduced from 18% to 15%. In October 2008, this filter helped to avoid the single largest loss of a naïve strategy's -35%. Similarly, during the second European credit crisis in July 2011, it helped to filter out a large loss of 37% in a single month so that the largest monthly loss is reduced to merely 4%. Overall Sharpe ratio is increased from 0.65 for a naïve strategy to 0.88. Again, all results here are net of transaction cost assumed to be 0.6% per month.

Table 1-8 Performance Statistics of U.S. 10-Year Swap Rate One-Month Volatility Premium Investment (Naïve Strategy vs. Vol Curve Filter, January 2001–June 2013)

	Average Annualized Return in %		Annualized Standard Deviation of Return in %		Maximal One Month Loss In %		Sharpe Ratio	
	Naïve	Vol Curve Filter	Naïve	Vol Curve Filter	Naïve	Vol Curve Filter	Naïve	Vol Curve Filter
2001	11.01	-3.73	17.96	12.46	-11.47	-11.47	0.61	-0.30
2002	47.41	38.30	17.69	16.58	-3.37	-2.32	2.68	2.31
2003	16.19	12.67	21.11	15.76	-7.10	-7.10	0.77	0.80
2004	31.94	10.32	12.13	6.71	-1.78	-1.78	2.63	1.54
2005	5.65	8.06	8.53	7.28	-4.19	-4.19	0.66	1.11
2006	3.68	2.23	8.24	5.15	-4.05	-4.05	0.45	0.43
2007	-27.08	1.43	18.64	8.64	-10.35	-7.39	-1.45	0.17
2008	-5.03	-10.86	57.39	22.12	-34.65	-19.75	-0.09	-0.49
2009	73.71	56.12	29.92	25.31	-8.19	-7.80	2.46	2.22
2010	-8.94	-13.07	28.90	19.34	-13.63	-13.63	-0.31	-0.68
2011	14.29	50.06	45.04	17.94	-36.59	-4.01	0.32	2.79
2012-2013	26.38	14.15	24.65	22.87	-17.55	-17.55	1.07	0.62
Total	18.13	15.21	27.88	17.22	-36.59	-19.75	0.65	0.88

Source: Bloomberg

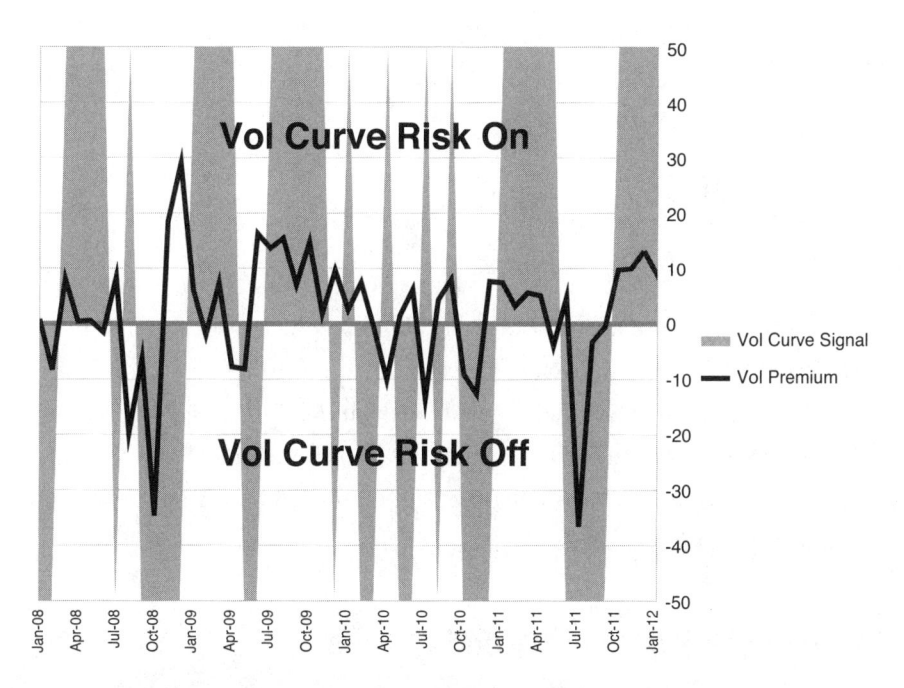

Figure 1-18 Vol curve filtering for U.S. one-month, 10-year swaptions

Together and Stronger: Applying Both Filters

Combining the two rules into a hybridized strategy again leads to a strategy greater than the sum of its parts. What happens when you combine both GARCH and vol curve filters to the naïve strategy? Table 1-9 and Figure 1-19 reveal the results. GARCH utilizes the past information and provides a scientific indication for the future actual volatility, and the vol curve tells us how options market prices the future uncertainty. By applying both filters, you reduced the large losses typically experienced in volatility premium investing such as in 2008 and 2011, and Sharpe ratio is increased from 0.65 to 0.94.

Compared with other risky benchmarks for the same period from 2001 to 2013, this rule based rates vol strategy outperforms, in risk adjusted basis, U.S. and global equity and high yield bonds. The correlations between rule based U.S. rates vol and the benchmark indices are close to zero (ranging from 0.03 to 0.07), making for an excellent addition to any portfolio. This is a winning performance from which many fund managers would expect to receive significant fees and compensation, yet here it was achieved by simply revisiting trades once a month, quickly assessing two filters, and following the rules on whether to keep risk on or get out—and that is all the active management it required.

Building a Volatility Portfolio

After applying simple filters to three liquid volatility markets, let's next discuss a volatility portfolio that is equally weighted with the three strategies that combine GARCH and market implied data already presented. You can compare the performance of the vol basket with relevant benchmarks: U.S. equity, Global equity, and U.S. and Global high yield credit. In addition, you can measure this rule based strategy performance against the Barclay Systematic Trader index, which averages 466 professional managers, with a systematic trading style as opposed to a discretionary one.

Table 1-9 Performance Statistics of U.S. 10-Year Swap Rate One-Month Volatility Premium Investment (Naïve Strategy vs. Joint Filter, January 2001–June 2013)

	Average Annualized Return in %		Annualized Standard Deviation of Return in %		Maximal One Month Loss in %		Sharpe Ratio	
	Naïve	Joint Filter	Naïve	Joint Filter	Naïve	Joint Filter	Naïve	Joint Filter
2001	11.01	4.72	17.96	1.09	-11.47	0.16	0.61	4.35
2002	47.41	40.76	17.69	15.85	-3.37	0.14	2.68	2.57
2003	16.19	16.80	21.11	13.10	-7.10	-3.42	0.77	1.28
2004	31.94	10.32	12.13	6.71	-1.78	-1.78	2.63	1.54
2005	5.65	9.77	8.53	3.36	-4.19	0.23	0.66	2.91
2006	3.68	2.90	8.24	5.16	-4.05	-4.05	0.45	0.56
2007	-27.08	-0.55	18.64	8.29	-10.35	-7.39	-1.45	-0.07
2008	-5.03	-11.02	57.39	22.11	-34.65	-19.75	-0.09	-0.50
2009	73.71	42.47	29.92	23.65	-8.19	-7.80	2.46	1.80
2010	-8.94	0.58	28.90	13.67	-13.63	-10.09	-0.31	0.04
2011	14.29	40.34	45.04	17.28	-36.59	-4.01	0.32	2.34
2012-2013	26.38	5.41	24.65	22.91	-17.55	-17.55	1.07	0.24
Total	18.13	14.26	27.88	15.23	-36.59	-19.75	0.65	0.94

Source: Bloomberg

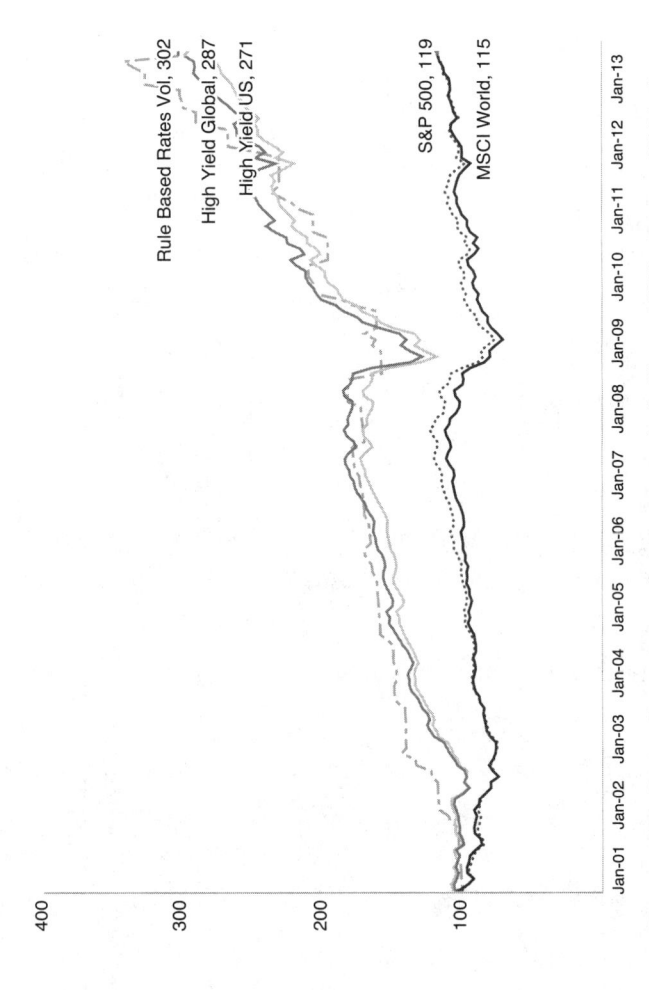

Figure 1-19 Risk adjusted cumulative returns (volatility = 10%), January 2001–June 2013

The way you invest in a volatility portfolio is by each month equally weighting the three volatility strategies. If any vol strategy is risk off, meaning the rules tell you not to invest, you underinvest; that is, you do not reallocate the risk to the remaining strategies. If all three vol strategies are risk off, (which itself is a powerful risk indicator to other risky investments), you do not invest at all. Like before, the transaction cost is assumed to be 0.4% for USDJPY vol, 1.5% for S&P 500 vol, and 0.6% for U.S. 10-year rates vol.

This volatility portfolio outperformed all five benchmarks. Tables 1-10, 1-11, and 1-12 report detailed performance statistics, and Figure 1-20 illustrates risk-adjusted cumulative returns. In particular, the correlations with the benchmarks are very low: 0.15 with S&P 500, 0.16 with MSCI world equity index, 0.18 with U.S. High Yield index, and 0.17 with Global High Yield index. It also has a low correlation with Systematic Trader Index which is -0.06. With these low correlations, volatility deserves its recognition as a separate asset class. You are encouraged to use this performance as a benchmark when evaluating any volatility related financial products.

Table 1-10 Average Annualized Returns of Volatility Premium Investment vs. Benchmarks, in %, January 2001–June 2013

	Naïve Volatility Basket	Rule based Volatility Basket	S&P 500	MSCI World Equity Index	High Yield U.S.	High Yield Global	Systematic Trader Index
2001	24.33	5.30	-12.07	-17.94	5.86	2.77	3.54
2002	12.55	14.98	-24.35	-21.67	-0.73	4.75	12.16
2003	28.41	23.65	24.22	27.83	25.86	28.60	8.98
2004	21.16	13.93	8.88	12.44	10.67	12.55	0.88
2005	5.43	7.33	3.24	7.62	2.82	3.63	1.14
2006	10.00	7.51	12.99	16.88	11.27	12.94	2.27
2007	-12.91	2.33	3.90	7.27	2.03	3.28	8.61
2008	-30.65	-0.99	-45.45	-50.61	-27.66	-28.31	17.18
2009	62.78	37.47	23.58	26.63	47.51	48.22	-3.29
2010	25.53	20.21	13.80	11.10	14.40	14.32	7.75
2011	17.33	25.87	1.15	-6.47	5.28	3.64	-3.65
2012-2013	17.87	8.71	18.71	13.71	8.90	9.12	-1.84
Total	16.21	14.30	2.81	2.67	9.09	9.97	4.18

Source: Bloomberg

Table 1-11 Annualized Return Standard Deviations of Volatility Premium Investment vs. Benchmarks, in %, January 2001–June 2013

	Naïve Volatility Basket	Rule based Volatility Basket	S&P 500	MSCI World Equity Index	High Yield U.S.	High Yield Global	Systematic Trader Index
2001	11.65	0.79	19.85	18.20	12.43	10.72	11.32
2002	11.09	5.81	20.61	19.30	12.15	12.23	12.35
2003	10.08	4.44	11.39	12.26	5.83	6.43	11.48
2004	6.41	3.99	7.25	8.19	4.02	4.96	8.63
2005	3.81	2.22	7.81	8.19	5.06	4.64	6.47
2006	5.03	1.87	5.70	7.45	2.28	2.97	6.46
2007	11.38	6.49	9.69	9.33	6.16	5.91	6.95
2008	37.73	11.94	20.99	23.63	21.68	22.82	9.08
2009	13.64	10.04	22.31	23.27	13.03	12.43	5.58
2010	16.80	8.44	19.31	20.60	7.17	9.57	6.69
2011	25.99	10.59	15.97	17.67	9.55	11.06	7.35
2012-2013	10.62	8.81	9.25	11.38	4.88	6.39	5.64
Total	16.89	7.69	15.67	16.53	10.67	11.12	8.28

Source: Bloomberg

Table 1-12 Annualized Sharpe Ratios of Volatility Premium Investment vs. Benchmarks, January 2001–June 2013

	Naïve Volatility Basket	Rule based Volatility Basket	S&P 500	MSCI World Equity Index	High Yield U.S.	High Yield Global	Systematic Trader Index
2001	2.09	6.73	-0.61	-0.99	0.47	0.26	0.31
2002	1.13	2.58	-1.18	-1.12	-0.06	0.39	0.98
2003	2.82	5.33	2.13	2.27	4.44	4.45	0.78
2004	3.30	3.49	1.23	1.52	2.66	2.53	0.10
2005	1.42	3.30	0.41	0.93	0.56	0.78	0.18
2006	1.99	4.02	2.28	2.27	4.95	4.36	0.35
2007	-1.13	0.36	0.40	0.78	0.33	0.55	1.24
2008	-0.81	-0.08	-2.17	-2.14	-1.28	-1.24	1.89
2009	4.60	3.73	1.06	1.14	3.65	3.88	-0.59
2010	1.52	2.39	0.71	0.54	2.01	1.50	1.16
2011	0.67	2.44	0.07	-0.37	0.55	0.33	-0.50
2012-2013	1.68	0.99	2.02	1.20	1.82	1.43	-0.33
Total	0.96	1.86	0.18	0.16	0.85	0.90	0.50

Source: Bloomberg

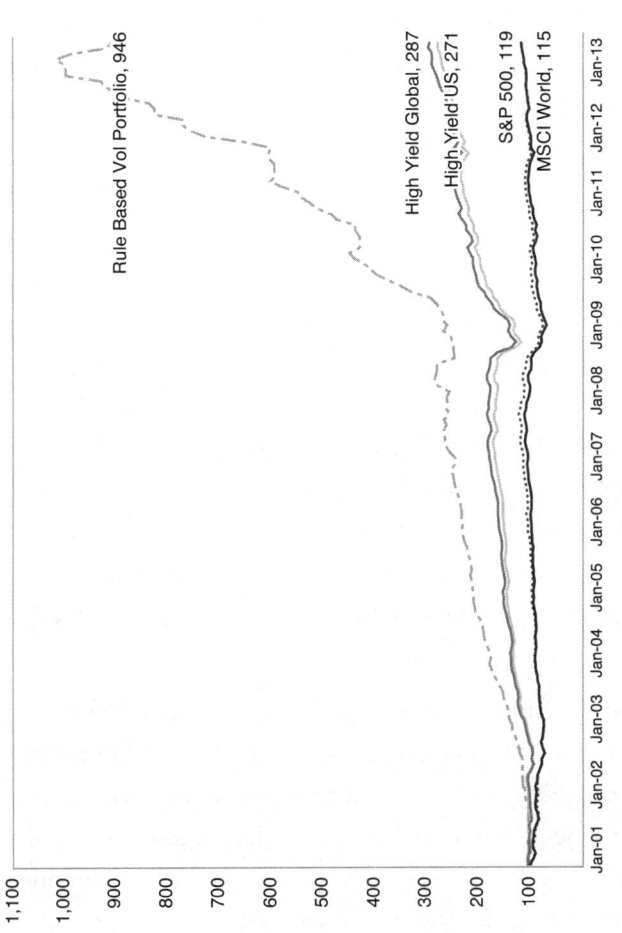

Figure 1-20 Cumulative Returns (volatility = 10%), January 2001–June 2013

Some Remarks

Between late 2008 and 2011 I visited countless institutional investors around the world and discussed with them their challenges and needs. Obviously volatility was the hot topic right after the financial crises. I always reminded the investors that those vol funds that focus only on long vol or only on short vol had a hard time surviving 2008 and 2009. The short vol funds had a tough time in 2008, immediately after a crisis is when volatility is the best performing strategy. Although the market bounces back, the psychology of the participants is still calibrated to the crisis. Recently scarred by market turmoil they are willing to pay high premiums for protection from further downside.

To survive in the long term, investing in only a single asset class won't work. With risky assets increasingly correlated, diversification is the key, and yet it is increasingly challenging. Still the natural tendency of investors and market participants is to focus in on the particular market they feel that they "know," often to the exclusion of others, because it is hard to be an expert in every market and asset class—hence the promotion here of rule based investment strategies for investors. The ease of use and implementation results in a broad, flexible ability to diversify, which is the foundation of a profitable, long-term investment strategy.

Although using VIX as a global risk indicator has long been adopted by the financial industry, recent academic research in the direction of "model-free" variance risk premium has produced exciting results. The difference between implied variance and realized variance is the variance risk premium. Traditionally we depended on the Black-Scholes formula to model this relationship, which is flawed as it assumes asset prices follow an idealized model. Beginning with the research of Carr and Madan,[13] as well as others, model free implied

---

[13] Carr, Peter and Dilip Madan. "Towards a Theory of Volatility Trading." Chapter 29 in *Volatility: New Estimation Techniques for Pricing Derivatives*. London: Risk Books, 1998.

vol/variance is computed from option prices without the use of a specific pricing model. If we use this model-free variance as our implied variance and high frequency data to compute the realized variance, as Bollersleve, Tauchen, and Zhou demonstrated,[14] the resulting difference is the variance/vol risk premium, which can be used to predict stock returns better than popular variables currently used such as the Profit/Earning ratio and the Profit/Debt ratio. This is an area of study with enormous potential that is ripe for exploration in the near future.

---

[14] Bollerslev, Tim, George Tauchen, and Hao Zhou. "Expected Stock Returns and Variance Risk Premia." *Review of Financial Studies* 22 (11) (November 2009): 4463–4492.

2

Rule Based Carry and Momentum Investment

Rule Based Carry Investment

This chapter is about the effectiveness of applying simple rules to the carry investment. The carry trade will be defined, a "benchmark" established, and finally rule based carry strategies will be discussed to improve returns and reduce risk.

A *carry trade* broadly means receiving returns from holding (*going long*) one asset against borrowing (*shorting*) another asset. For interest rates, this involves borrowing at low rates such as the overnight rate and lending or receiving long-term rates such as 30-year rates, assuming an upward sloping yield curve. This is known as *positive carry* because the net position is profitable to hold. The inverse position of receiving short-term rates and paying long-term rates is *negative carry* because it is held at a loss.

The focus in this chapter is on positive carry to achieve the goal of stable returns while minimizing risks. Negative carry, similar to shorting a stock, is a speculative high-risk strategy where the expectation of a dramatic repricing of assets would compensate for the losses of passively holding an unprofitable position. The pursuit of a reliable and reproducible investment strategy that operates on the basis of rules with minimal management, involves studying and improving positive carry trades rather than focusing on negative carry positions.

In financial markets, the term *carry trade* is generally understood to refer to investments in currency markets. It consists of borrowing in currencies (funding currency) with low interest rates to buy and hold currencies (target currency) with high interest rates. In this sense it is interest rate arbitrage between currency pairs. In a fixed income environment of low interest rates, carry trades in currencies provide an opportunity for higher returns in a high liquidity market. The investment will be profitable as long as target currency does not weaken against funding currency too greatly to erase the interest rate differential.

Since 2009 to the present in late 2013, the U.S. Federal Reserve has been keeping interest rates low. As a result, borrowing at the low rate of the U.S. dollars and investing in a higher interest rate currencies, such as the Australian dollar, yields an attractive return. At the end of August 2013, it was possible to earn around 2.6% carry per year through AUDUSD one month forward contracts because the exchange rate of Australian Dollar against U.S. dollar did not substantially weaken.

Now, in late 2013, it is not only the U.S. Federal Reserve that has been conducting an expansionary monetary policy; most developed countries are on the same track. Figures 2-1 and 2-2 describe the long history of Fed Funds Rates and U.K.'s Bank of England's Official Bank Rates. With the global economy still in recovery, interest rates are at historically unprecedented low levels. "Safe" investments have become inert investment, requiring even those seeking meager returns to turn to risky assets such as equities, high yield, and carry.

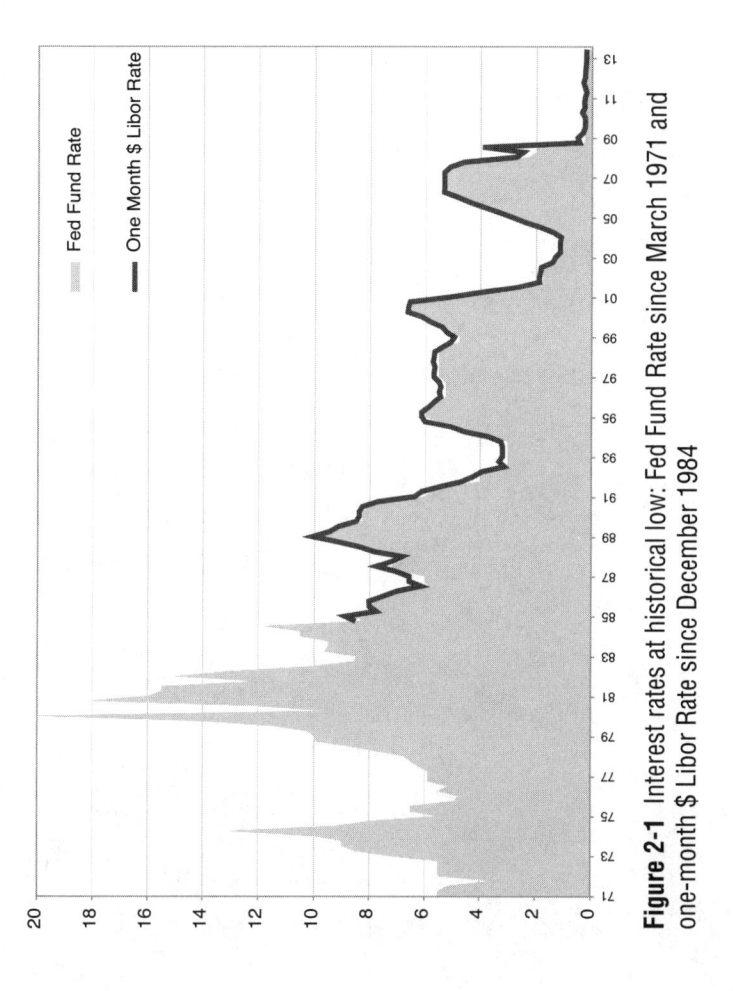

CHAPTER 2 • RULE BASED CARRY AND MOMENTUM INVESTMENT   81

Figure 2-1 Interest rates at historical low: Fed Fund Rate since March 1971 and one-month $ Libor Rate since December 1984

82 Rule Based Investing

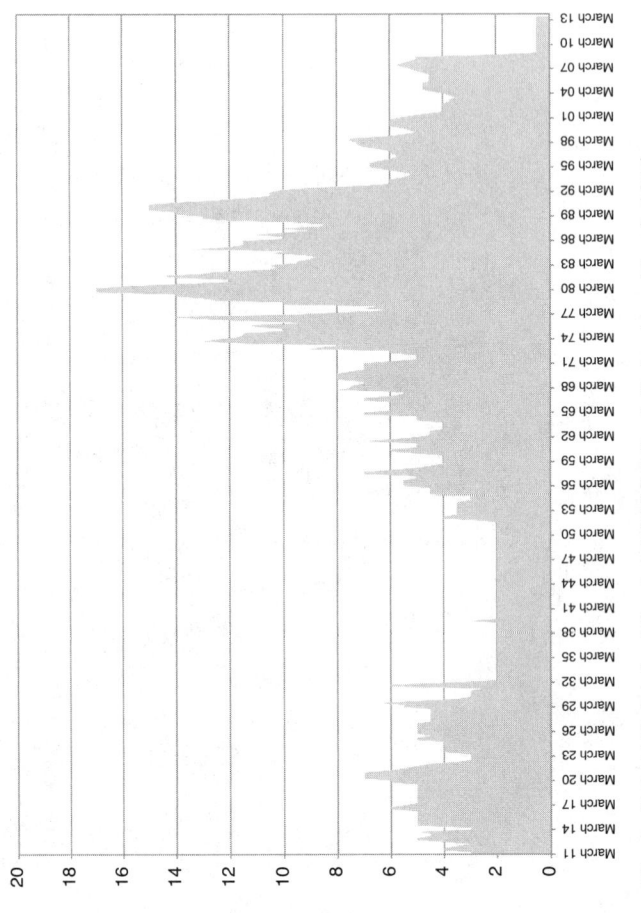

Figure 2-2 U.K. Bank of England Official Bank Rate since March 1911

"Benchmark" Returns in the FX Carry Trade

Given the ever-present exchange rate risk, what kind of returns should you expect an overall FX carry trade strategy to generate? Has the FX carry trade been profitable over the past decade? Certainly you seek a greater return than the risk-free rate on U.S. Treasuries; however, is the FX carry more or less attractive when compared with other risky investments such as investing in the stock market or the U.S. high yield bond market?

A benchmark currency carry investment is needed to illustrate in greater detail the profitability versus the risk of investing in the simplest form of the carry strategy. Let's use the U.S. Dollar as the base currency against the nine most liquid foreign currencies (Australia Dollar, Canadian Dollar, Swiss Franc, Euro, British Pound, Japanese Yen, Norwegian Krone, New Zealand Dollar, and Swedish Krona). The rule is that on the monthly basis, you create an equally weighted basket such that if the interest rate of the foreign currency is higher than U.S. rate, you borrow one U.S. Dollar and buy and hold the foreign currency for a month. If the interest rate of the foreign currency is lower than U.S. rate, you borrow one U.S. dollar worth of foreign currency and buy and hold the U.S. dollar for a month. Note that these trades are always positive carry, where you net receive interest rates for holding the position. This investment is "net of funding" because the borrowing cost is taken into account. The return is therefore excess return.

This is a simple and inexpensive strategy to implement; Table 2-1 summarizes the resulting profitability of this buy-and-hold carry trade since January 2001. At first glance, the result is promising: over thirteen years, simple carry strategies, averaging among G10 currencies returned on the average 3.5% per year, with a Sharpe ratio of 0.31. This is higher than buy-and-hold in the S&P 500 over the same period, which returned 2.8% per year with a Sharpe ratio less than 0.18. Out of the nine currencies against the U.S. Dollar, seven achieved positive returns with the carry strategy, with Swedish Krona returns the highest at 8.59% per year.

Table 2-1 Performance Statistics of Individual Currency Carry Against the U.S. Dollar (January 2001–June 2013)

	AUD	CAD	CHF	EUR	GBP	JPY	NOK	NZD	SEK	Average	S&P 500
Annualized Individual Carry Return in %											
2001-2007	8.55	3.11	-3.14	6.16	3.32	2.97	4.06	10.47	9.62	5.0	2.40
2008	-15.90	-13.60	-6.39	7.37	-12.20	-19.08	-21.46	-22.30	1.96	-11.3	-45.45
2009	28.52	-19.34	-3.46	1.03	11.08	2.14	19.73	26.37	9.62	8.4	23.58
2010-2013	-3.38	-2.56	1.20	4.10	-2.34	10.97	-2.76	0.44	0.47	0.7	12.86
Total	7.34	-0.55	-3.37	6.24	2.27	0.77	2.28	7.57	8.59	3.5	2.81
Annualized Individual Carry Standard Deviation in %											
2001-2007	10.41	7.91	8.82	8.13	7.31	8.46	10.00	10.96	9.79	9.1	13.03
2008	22.34	14.09	18.99	17.31	14.40	11.97	16.29	16.50	16.83	16.5	20.99
2009	17.34	15.40	12.48	13.73	11.41	13.48	9.19	22.45	17.96	14.8	22.31
2010-2013	14.41	8.25	12.55	11.58	8.72	8.77	13.03	14.21	12.14	11.5	14.13
Total	13.70	9.64	11.34	10.68	8.95	9.69	11.85	13.74	12.15	11.3	15.67
Sharpe Ratio											
2001-2007	0.82	0.39	-0.36	0.76	0.45	0.35	0.41	0.95	0.98	0.55	0.18
2008	-0.71	-0.97	-0.34	0.43	-0.85	-1.59	-1.32	-1.35	0.12	-0.68	-2.17
2009	1.64	-1.26	-0.28	0.07	0.97	0.16	2.15	1.17	0.54	0.57	1.06
2010-2013	-0.23	-0.31	0.10	0.35	-0.27	1.25	-0.21	0.03	0.04	0.06	0.91
Total	0.54	-0.06	-0.30	0.58	0.25	0.08	0.19	0.55	0.71	0.31	0.18

Source: Bloomberg

Figure 2-3 compares the risk-adjusted performance of nine carry trades against the U.S. Dollar as well as the S&P 500 from January 2001 to June 2013. To get a fairer picture of the performance, you can adjust the returns by normalizing volatility to an annualized 10%. Six out of nine currency carry trades outperformed the S&P 500.

More important than greater returns alone is the higher Sharpe ratio of carry trades and returns that are less skewed. Moreover, returns of carry trades are relatively uncorrelated with returns from other risky assets such as the S&P 500. As described earlier, the Sharpe ratio is a measure of the risk-adjusted performance of an investment. What skew tells us is that if the market goes down, the value of an asset also goes down to an even greater degree. A high kurtosis value tells us that there is a greater chance of extreme outcomes than a bell curve of normal distribution would suggest. The average G10 carry exhibits higher kurtosis than the S&P 500.

Table 2-2 goes into greater detail in comparing the return statistics of each currency carry trade (against the U.S. Dollar) to the S&P 500. You can see that the average return of a carry trade in nine developed currencies has significantly better skew and kurtosis profiles. The average correlation is as low as 0.2 with the S&P 500. This result should offer investors a "baseline" scenario or "benchmark" in investing in Foreign Exchange when selecting fund managers or investment products. When considering an equity fund manager, it's good to compare the returns and correlations of the fund's performance against the S&P 500 index. When selecting a currency fund manager, you should compare the performance and correlations against Table 2-2 to be certain that the particular fund manager did indeed generate value to justify the fees required for investing in the fund. Figure 2-4 displays the risk adjusted cumulative returns of G10 carry trade compared with S&P 500.

Figure 2-3 Risk-adjusted cumulative returns of G10 carry versus S&P 500 (volatility = 10%)

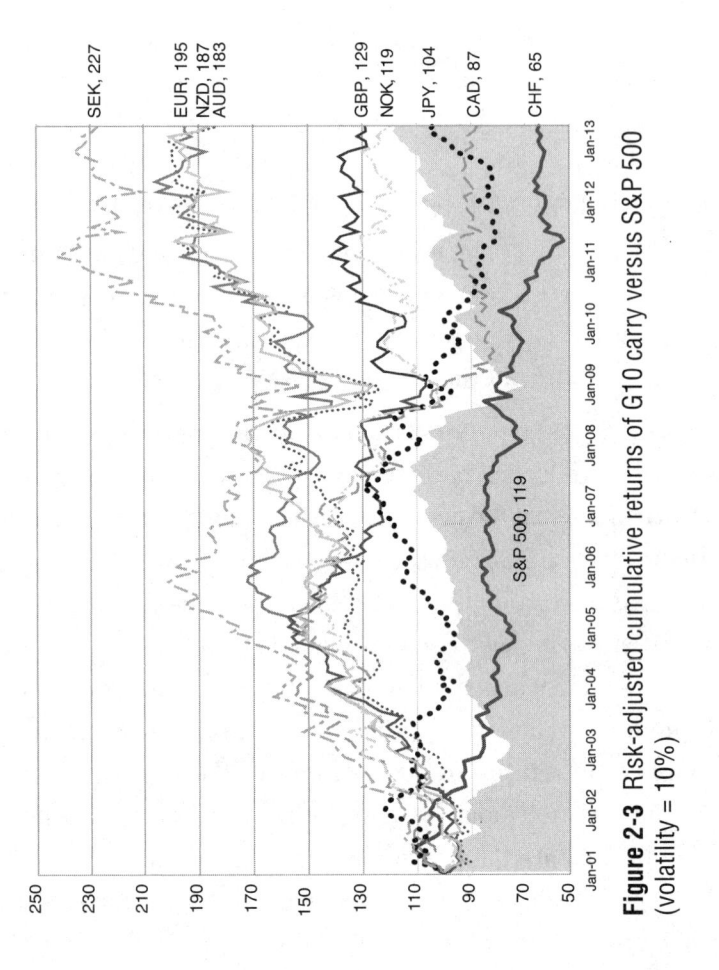

Table 2-2 Performance Statistics of Individual Currency Carry Against the U.S. Dollar (January 2001–June 2013)

	AUD	CAD	CHF	EUR	GBP	JPY	NOK	NZD	SEK	Avg	S&P 500
Max. One-Month Loss in %	-15.5	-12.2	-13.5	-9.5	-9.4	-7.2	-12.7	-12.8	-7.6	-11.2	-16.9
Skew of Monthly Return	-0.59	-1.03	-0.21	-0.02	-0.27	0.28	-0.54	-0.40	0.11	-0.3	-0.63
Kurtosis of Monthly Return	1.79	2.44	1.97	1.09	1.76	0.11	1.08	1.69	0.35	1.4	1.03
Correlation with S&P 500	0.61	0.25	-0.18	0.11	0.14	0.14	0.37	0.53	0.19	0.2	

Source: Bloomberg

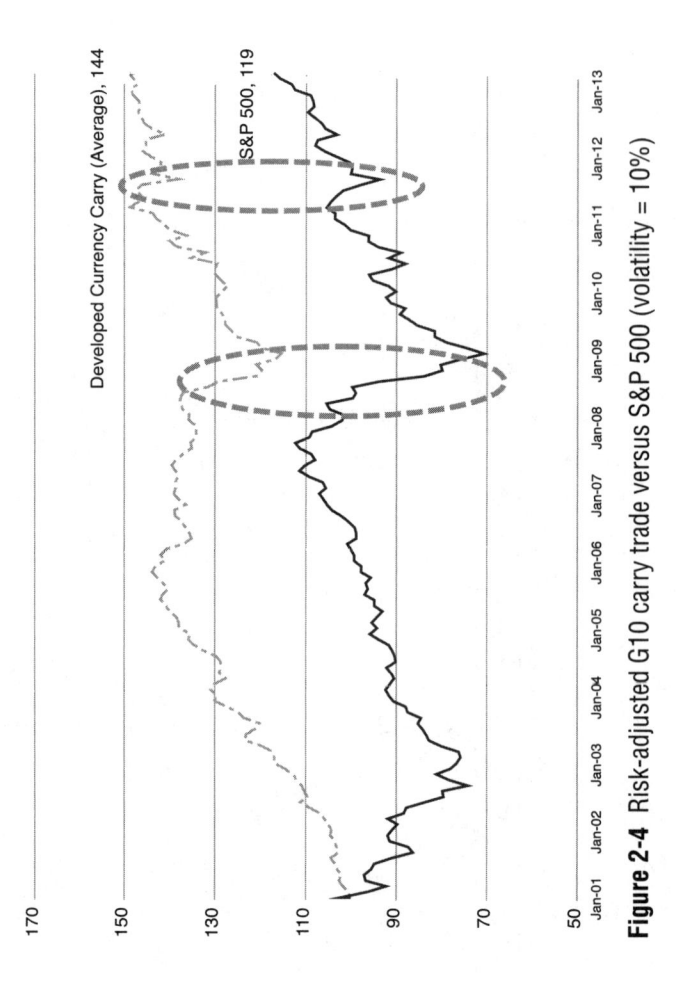

Figure 2-4 Risk-adjusted G10 carry trade versus S&P 500 (volatility = 10%)

The Risks of the FX Carry Trade

The average excess return of 3.5%, with a Sharpe ratio exceeding that of the stock market, makes the carry trade a very attractive investment. The risk that underlies the returns, however, is that exchange rates can move in a volatile and dramatic fashion. To draw from recent history, one of the most popular funding currencies is the Japanese Yen as a result of the Japanese Central Bank having kept its interest rates low for decades. With a minimal return from savings accounts, currency trading became extremely popular with average citizens. *The New York Times* published an article, "Japanese Housewives Sweat in Secret as Markets Reel," on September 16, 2007: "Until the credit crisis, which began with troubles in the American mortgage market, the value of foreign currencies traded online by private Japanese citizens, including women, averaged $9.1 billion a day—almost a fifth of all foreign exchange trading worldwide during trading hours in Tokyo."

This was the height of Yen carry trade. From August 2008 to January 2009, AUDJPY lost 43%, and other frequently traded carry pairs such as the New Zealand Dollar and the British Pound against the Yen, lost 42% and 39%, respectively. Needless to say, whatever carry was being received from the interest rate deferential was crushed by the sudden and brutal move in the exchange rate. Figure 2-5 illustrates the history of AUDJPY, NZDJPY and GBPJPY from 2000 to 2013. The sudden plunge in 2008 of these three currency pairs is a reminder of how volatile currency market can be.

The Steam Roller

Figure 2-6 illustrates how volatile carry strategies can be. Warren Buffet once said that the carry trade is like picking up the nickels before the steam roller, meaning that receiving the moderate returns of the carry trade came with the risk of being destroyed by a dramatic shift in exchange rates, as certainly was the case with AUDJPY in autumn of 2008.

90 RULE BASED INVESTING

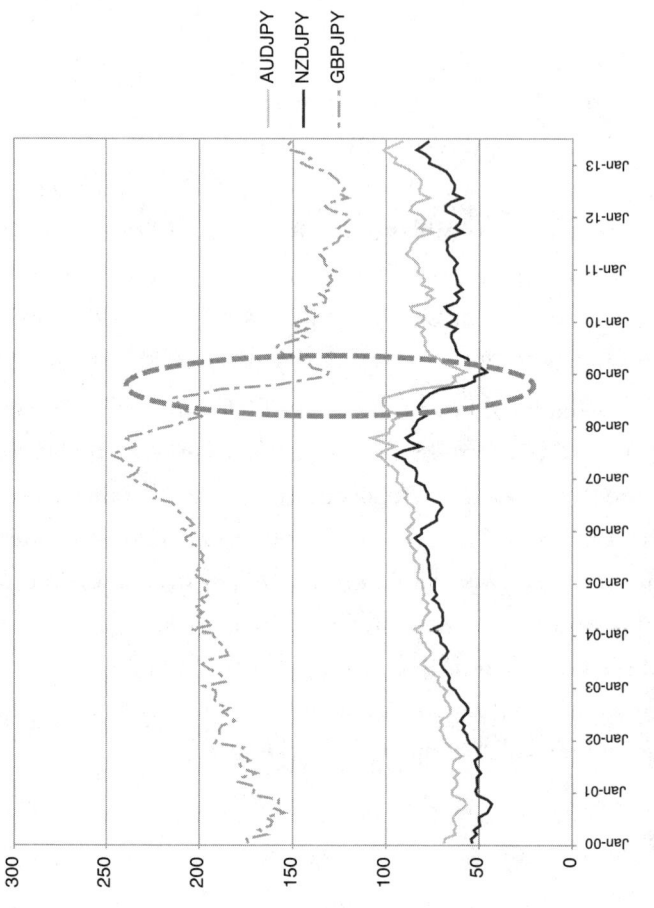

Figure 2-5 Popular carry trades during crises

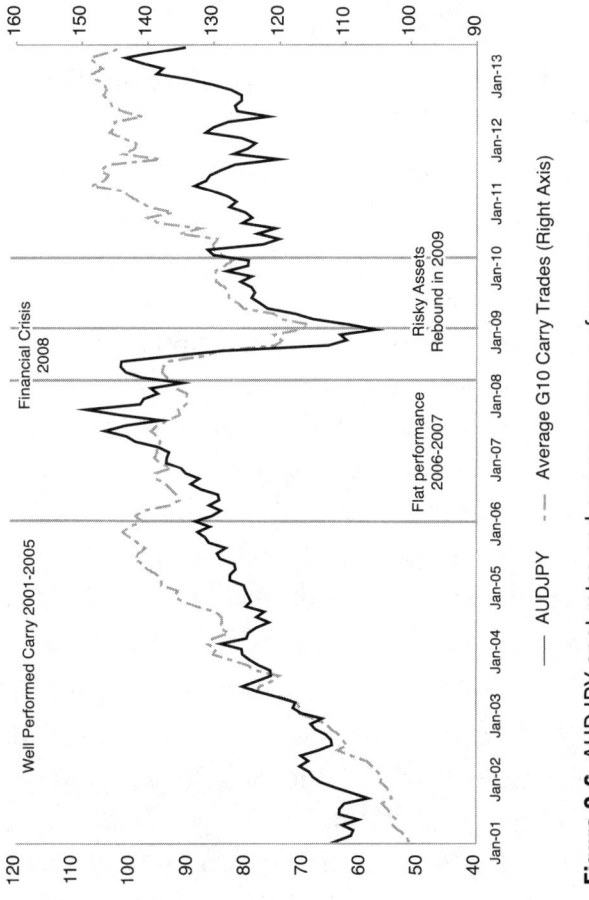

Figure 2-6 AUDJPY spot rates and average carry performance

There are several important observations to be drawn from Figure 2-6. The first is to note the high correlation of the popular AUDJPY pair and the average G10 carry basket across several different periods over previous years. From 2001 to 2005 the carry trade was highly profitable. There was a period near the end of 2005 where the carry trade was flat or incurred some losses. In 2008 the carry trade suffered significant losses, and 2009 was marked by the rebound of risky assets including carry. The G10 basket is consistently less volatile than the individual AUDJPY pair, particularly as the basket experienced a significantly lower draw-down during the financial crisis.

The draw-down of the carry strategy is substantial, meaning a steep plunge in value is a real and present danger. A notable example is that during the 2008 crisis, AUDJPY experienced a one-month draw-down of more than 25%, an enormous price movement for a major currency pair. What happened is that the carry trade has a tendency to become crowded as many investors position themselves to profit from the positive returns. Typical carry trades have been highly leveraged to amplify returns, creating greater investor urgency to exit losing positions. When the trade begins to weaken, investors flee in droves, causing a dramatic swing in exchange rates. This stampede of capital creates significant unwind risk for carry trades. In a frantic market environment bid/ask spreads widen, with investors willing to cover their positions at heavy losses in order to take risk off.

Popular carry trades have become highly correlated with other risky assets, such as the S&P 500 and the U.S. high yield credit market, and correlation tends to further increase during a crisis. For example from January 2001 to June 2013, AUDJPY spot return had a correlation of 0.61 with the S&P 500 and 0.54 with Barclays Capital's U.S. High Yield Index. During 2008 the correlation increased to 0.75 with S&P and 0.81 with U.S. High Yield Index. Figure 2-7 illustrates the co-movements among these risky investments. Take note of this correlation as you pursue indicators of market anxiety to serve as an early warning system.

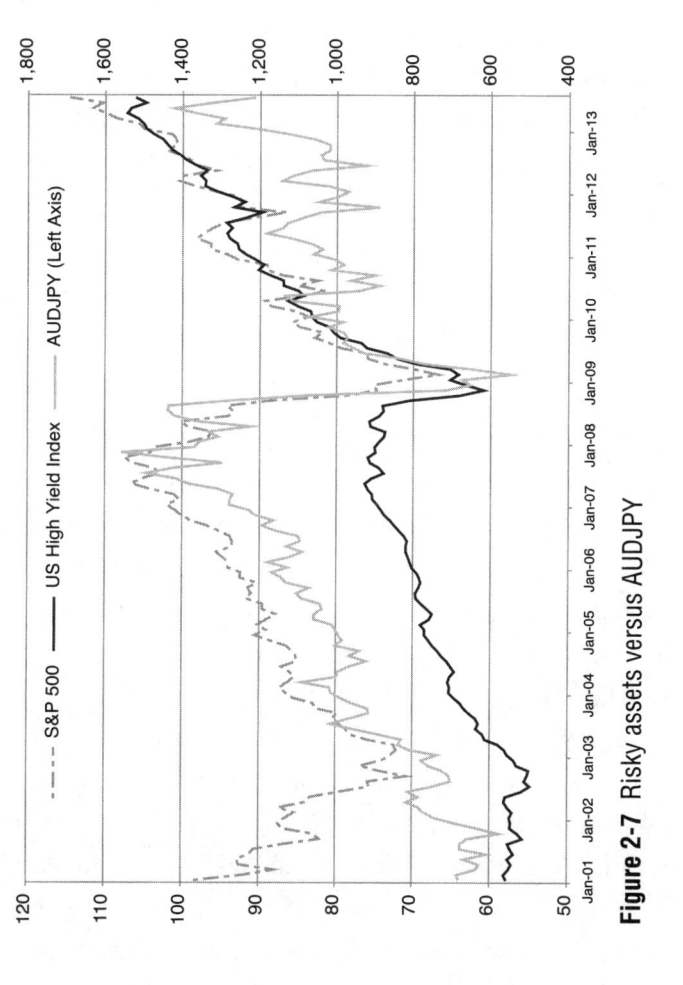

Figure 2-7 Risky assets versus AUDJPY

Simple yet Effective Rules for Carry Investment

The ground is trembling. Faced with the threat of an approaching steam roller, what is needed is an early alert system. The following sections provide three simple and easy-to-implement strategies to avoid oncoming danger, although there does exist other means of obtaining similar results. The first rule is diversification across currencies. The second rule is to use the VIX (implied volatility of S&P 500 options) as a market indicator of trouble. The third is to use a simple Momentum strategy as a hedge against carry. The ease with which these strategies are implemented and their effectiveness is so pronounced that the application of these strategies should serve as reference point against which to compare professional returns.

Diversification

The popular single carry strategy is highly risky. In previous sections graphs revealed the drastic move of currency pairs such as AUDJPY. The annualized volatility of the carry returns from G9 currencies against the U.S. Dollar ranges from 9% to 14%. As was the case with the simplest single currency buy-and-hold carry trade discussed earlier in the chapter, you build a diversified carry portfolio with the nine most liquid currencies (G9) against the U.S. Dollar: the Australian Dollar, Canadian Dollar, Swiss Franc, Euro, British Pound, Japanese Yen, Norwegian Krone, New Zealand Dollar, and the Swedish Krona. By simply diversifying the investment, without doing anything fancy, the volatility of carry returns is reduced. To build a simple diversified portfolio, you invest an equal dollar amount in each of the nine currencies on a monthly basis. Buy currencies with positive carry, sell those with negative carry against the U.S. Dollar and hold the positions for a month.

The results are reported in Table 2-3: From January 2001 to June 2013, this simple diversified carry portfolio had a Sharpe ratio of 0.62, 50% higher than the average of individual carry trades. A diversified

G9 carry portfolio reduces the overall volatility to half, from an average of 11% to 5.5%.

Another way to build a diversified portfolio is to buy the top three currencies with highest interest rate differential and sell equal amounts of the bottom three currencies with lowest interest differential. In other words, even if a currency has a positive interest rate differential against the U.S. Dollar, if it's among the lowest, you still sell it. The long 3/short 3 carry portfolio can obtain a Sharpe ratio of 0.7.[1] Often long and short currencies at the same time with equal amount of U.S. Dollar are preferred because it is "dollar neutral," that is, the portfolio is invariant to the U.S. Dollar's up or down against other currencies.

Let's compare these two simple diversification carry strategies against S&P 500 and Barclay Currency Trader index, the latter representing the average performance of professional currency managers.[2] For the period between January 2001 and June 2013, with annualized returns of 3.5% and 2.8% and Sharpe ratios of 0.62 and 0.70, both diversified carry portfolios outperformed the S&P 500. Notably, with a Sharpe ratio of 0.71, the average professional FX trader did not significantly outperform these simple diversified carry portfolios. Figure 2-8 illustrates the historical performances of these two diversified carries against the S&P 500 and FX trader index, with volatility normalized to 10% per annum. Diversified carry portfolios can achieve a performance comparable to the average professional currency programs. Currency managers as a whole however, represented here by the FX trader index, does a remarkable job of minimizing downside: In 2008, the FX trader index gained 2.5%, whereas the S&P 500 lost

---

[1] Note that the result reported here are returns net of borrowing cost but not net of transaction cost.

[2] Barclay (not to be confused with Barlay's Capital) Currency Traders Index is an equal weighted composite of managed programs that trade currency futures and/or cash forwards in the inter-bank market. In 2013, 105 currency programs were included in the index.

more than 45%, and these two diversified carry portfolios lost 11.3% and 9.8%. The next section addresses this issue.

Table 2-3 Performance Summary of Simple Carry Investment vs. Benchmarks (January 2001–June 2013)

	Equally Weighted	Long 3/ Short 3	S&P 500	FX Trader Index
Annualized Average Return in %				
2001-2007	5.01	3.96	2.40	4.03
2008	-11.29	-9.81	-45.45	2.48
2009	8.41	10.74	23.58	2.06
2010-2013	0.68	1.52	12.86	1.97
Total	3.46	2.79	2.81	3.25
Annualized Return Standard Deviation in %				
2001-2007	3.83	3.29	13.03	6.03
2008	8.55	6.09	20.99	1.93
2009	6.43	4.46	22.31	1.52
2010-2013	6.38	4.22	14.13	2.34
Total	5.56	4.01	15.67	4.61
Sharpe Ratio				
2001-2007	1.31	1.20	0.18	0.67
2008	-1.32	-1.61	-2.17	1.29
2009	1.31	2.41	1.06	1.35
2010-2013	0.11	0.36	0.91	0.84
Total	0.62	0.70	0.18	0.71

Source: Bloomberg

VIX: Reading Market Indicators to Avoid the Steam Roller

Diversification helps to reduce downside risk but does not eliminate it. The second rule is to condition the carry trade on a "market indicator" such as the VIX. Why? In continuing with the steam roller analogy, when the ground starts to shake and the birds and animals scatter, it is time to stop picking up nickels before disaster rolls through. Of course the rumbling could be a heavy truck down the road or a herd of cattle, but why remain on the tracks and risk being flattened?

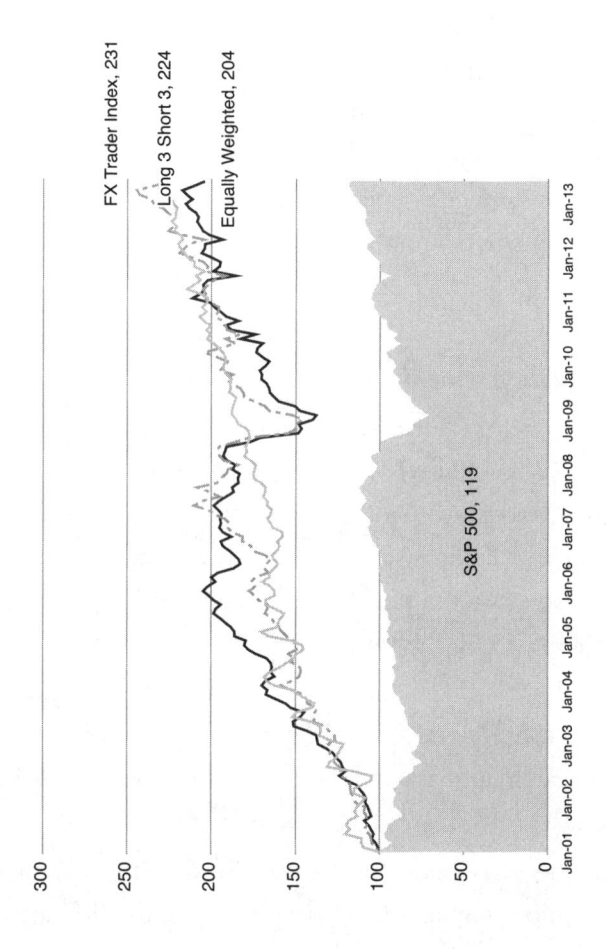

Figure 2-8 Risk-adjusted cumulative returns (volatility = 10%)

No one has perfect foresight of "when" a disaster will occur. When fear begins to spread among the market participants, however, especially the sophisticated players, you want to know about it. Rather than spending thousands dollars a year to subscribe to a complicated "risk indicator" newsletter or model, it is much easier and more effective to simply observe the behavior of the options market. The nature of options pricing is heavily quantitative and technical and typically employs some of the brightest minds on the trading floor. Options desks are well equipped to detect the slightest change in risk sentiment, and they act quickly on the slightest hint of trouble. When there is a spike in implied volatility, it means that the "fast money" is uneasy and nervous. High implied volatility is a warning to approach the market with caution.

You can implement the VIX filter through rules that switch the carry trade on and off conditional to the VIX.

Why does this indicator of stock market sentiment work for the FX carry trade? This is based on the important observation that during crises, risky trades are highly correlated. "Risky trades" include investing in stocks, FX, high yield credit, and other liquid assets where massive losses are always a possibility (in contrast to Treasuries and other "safe havens").

Of course there will be times and currency pairs that will not be as correlated to the S&P 500. Conditioning an FX carry trade on the VIX, however, can help you avoid the "super meltdown" global events such as the crash of 2008.

Switching the carry trade on/off conditional on the VIX produces remarkable results. Similar to the simple buy-and-hold carry trade discussed earlier in the chapter, you invest in the nine most liquid currencies (G9) against the U.S. Dollar. Once each month you look at the level of the VIX that prevailed at the close of previous trading day. If the level of the VIX the day before is higher than the 90th percentile of the past year's VIX levels, you do not enter a carry trade. If the previous day's VIX level is lower than the 90th percentile of the past year's VIX level, the carry trade is entered. You can apply VIX filter to these two diversified carry portfolios: equally weighted and long 3/short 3.

The performance of this simple conditional rule based carry trade is shown in Table 2-4. Compared to the simply diversified carry portfolio, the conditional strategy added more than 1% return per year, lowered volatility by 0.6% to 0.8% per year, and therefore achieved a Sharpe ratio above 1, close to a 40% increase. The benefit of overlaying the VIX filter is illustrated in Figure 2-9 which compares the risk adjusted cumulative returns of the two carry baskets with and without the filter.

Why is the improvement so drastic when the VIX filter is applied? The reason is that VIX conditioning has allowed the carry trade to avoid three crises over the past decade: the beginning of subprime crisis in 2007, the single largest financial crisis in 2008, and the European Union/Greek crisis in 2010. These crises spilled over across the globe very quickly with all risky assets suffering a collective meltdown. With VIX being the barometer of fear, by reading its extraordinarily high level (above 90th percentile), you would switch off the carry trade and put the money into cash or even a "safe haven" investment such as Treasuries or gold. Therefore, VIX is a useful global risk indicator not only for equity but also for other seemly uncorrelated risky assets such as high yield credit and FX carry trades. Figure 2-10 displays the timing and impact of the risk on/off signals on the performances of the equally weighted carry basket.

Table 2-4 Performance Summary of Carry Investment With and Without VIX Filter vs. Benchmarks (January 2001–June 2013)

	Equally Weighted	Long 3/Short 3	VIX overlaid Eq. Wgt.	VIX overlaid Long/short	S&P 500	FX Trader Index
Annualized Average Return in %						
2001-2007	5.01	3.96	5.39	3.83	2.40	4.03
2008	-11.29	-9.81	-3.27	-2.56	-45.45	2.48
2009	8.41	10.74	8.41	10.74	23.58	2.06
2010-2013	0.68	1.52	2.42	2.43	12.86	1.97
Total	3.46	2.79	4.83	3.80	2.81	3.25
Annualized Return Standard Deviation in %						
2001-2007	3.83	3.29	3.65	3.08	13.03	6.03
2008	8.55	6.09	4.50	3.40	20.99	1.93
2009	6.43	4.46	6.43	4.46	22.31	1.52
2010-2013	6.38	4.22	5.74	3.78	14.13	2.34
Total	5.56	4.01	4.76	3.38	15.67	4.61
Sharpe Ratio						
2001-2007	1.31	1.20	1.48	1.24	0.18	0.67
2008	-1.32	-1.61	-0.73	-0.75	-2.17	1.29
2009	1.31	2.41	1.31	2.41	1.06	1.35
2010-2013	0.14	0.36	0.42	0.64	1.20	1.11
Total	0.62	0.70	1.01	1.13	0.18	0.71

Source: Bloomberg

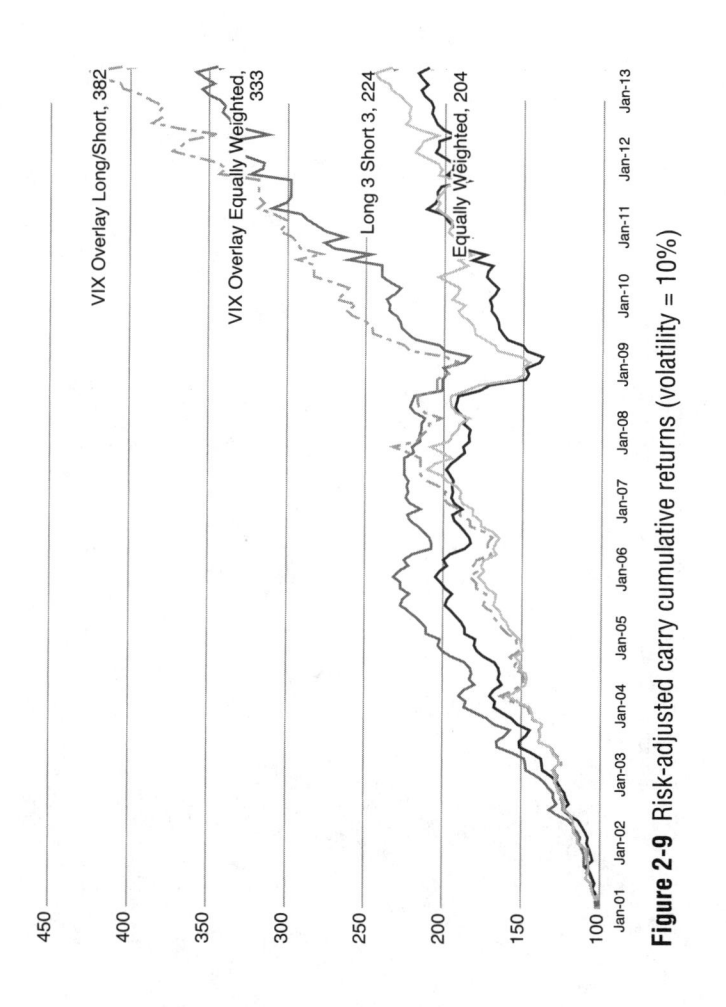

Figure 2-9 Risk-adjusted carry cumulative returns (volatility = 10%)

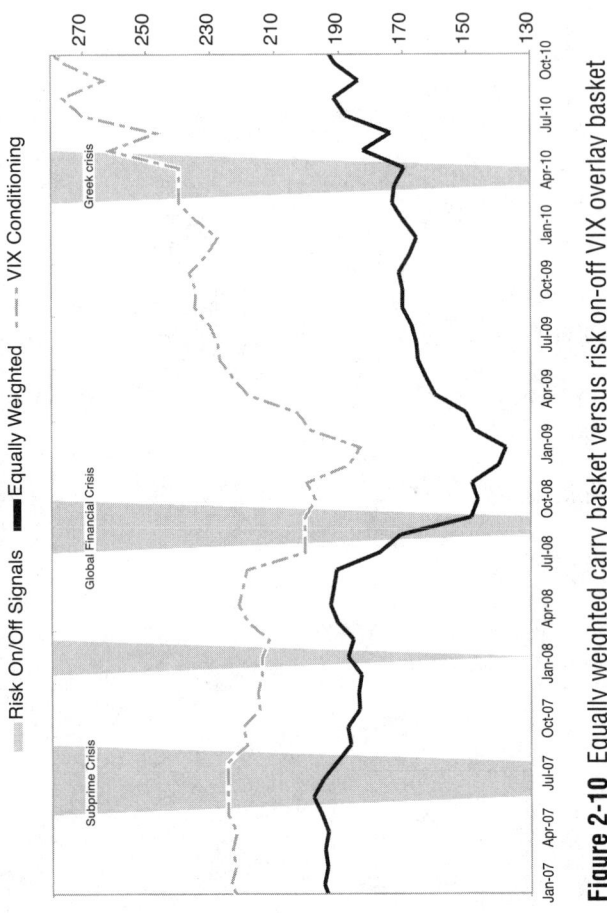

Figure 2-10 Equally weighted carry basket versus risk on-off VIX overlay basket (2007–2010)

The idea of conditioning the carry trade on the VIX has been documented in academic research by professionals such as Bhansali,[3] Melvin and Taylor,[4] and most recently De Bock and Filho.[5] Are there other indicators that can assist in risk on/off signaling? The answer is yes. Popular among professional currency traders, for example, is the TED Spread as discussed earlier, currency-specific volatility indices such as JP Morgan's Global FX Volatility Index, credit spreads, and the slope of the yield curve, among others. This book does not go into detail on the effectiveness of these other indicators; they merit a more complete discussion in a more advanced text.

Momentum Strategy as a Hedge for Carry Investment

A momentum strategy simply means buying assets that have produced positive returns in the past and selling those that have produced negative returns. As a "jump on the bandwagon" style of investing, momentum strategies are closely associated to trend following. Numerous academic studies have found that the momentum strategy is a good hedge for carry, not just for FX, but also for other risky asset classes such as equities and commodities.[6]

There are countless ways to build a momentum strategy, as a Google search will confirm. Simply speaking, the success of a momentum strategy relies on the predictability of future price movement based on historical prices. This is quite a bold principle as every investment disclaimer reminds us that the historical returns of a strategy do

---

[3] Bhansali, Vineer. "Volatility and the Carry Trade." *The Journal of Fixed Income* 3 (Winter 2007): 72–84.

[4] Melvin, Michael and Mark P. Taylor. "The Crisis in the Foreign Exchange Market." *Journal of International Money and Finances* 28 (December 2009): 1317–1330.

[5] De Bock, Reinout and Irineu de Carvalho Filho. "The Behavior of Currencies During Risk-Off Episode." IMF Paper, 2013.

[6] The following paper gives a thorough review of this area of research. Burnside, Craig, Martin Eichenbaum, and Sergio Rebelo. "Carry Trade and Momentum in Currency Markets." *Annual Review of Financial Economics*, Annual Reviews 3(1) (December 2011): 511–535.

not promise further success in the future. Momentum begs to differ. It argues that past performance often can be indicative of the future. The major difference among all of the possible variations of momentum strategies lies in the compression or representation of information extracted from past price movement. A popular momentum strategy for example, is a so-called *moving average cross-over*: You select a short window (for example, 5 days) and a long window (perhaps 200 days) moving average. It is believed that if the short-term moving average is higher than the long-term moving average, a buy signal is generated.

Because there are countless papers and books on momentum trading, for the purposes of demonstration only this discussion focuses on the simplest momentum strategy involving a moving average crossover. Each month you go long those currencies against the U.S. Dollar whose three-month returns are higher than their one-year returns, against selling those currencies with a three-month return lower than the one-year return. Looking through the lens of this strategy, over the period between January 2001 and June 2013, this momentum portfolio achieved an annualized return of 3.7%, volatility under 6%, and a Sharpe ratio of 0.64. More importantly, this simple momentum portfolio is negatively correlated with these two diversified carry strategies: -0.23 with equally weighted and -0.29 with long 3/short 3 carry portfolio. Given the similar magnitude of volatilities and low negative correlations, it is justified to build a 50/50 portfolio diversified between carry and momentum. Only the mix of long/short with momentum is shown for this demonstration. Unsurprisingly the resulting 50/50 blend of strategies achieves a greater Sharpe ratio of 1.08. Table 2-5 summarizes the performance statistics.

Figure 2-11 provides a clearer picture that the momentum strategy has been a good hedge for carry: Although carry suffered drastic losses during the 2008 Global Financial Crisis, momentum performed well by picking up the negative trend.

Table 2-5 Performance Summary of Carry Investment With and Without Momentum Hedge vs. Benchmarks (January 2001–June 2013)

	Long 3/Short 3	Momentum Only	Long 3/Short 3 within Momentum Hedge	S&P 500	FX Trader Index
Annualized Average Return in %					
2001-2007	3.96	1.06	2.51	2.40	4.03
2008	-9.81	11.12	0.66	-45.45	2.48
2009	10.74	16.57	13.66	23.58	2.06
2010-2013	1.52	0.49	1.00	12.86	1.97
Total	2.79	3.73	3.26	2.81	3.25
Annualized Return Standard Deviation in %					
2001-2007	3.29	4.27	2.62	13.03	6.03
2008	6.09	10.99	3.94	20.99	1.93
2009	4.46	5.17	3.68	22.31	1.52
2010-2013	4.22	6.04	2.84	14.13	2.34
Total	4.01	5.79	3.01	15.67	4.61
Sharpe Ratio					
2001-2007	1.20	0.25	0.96	0.18	0.67
2008	-1.61	1.01	0.17	-2.17	1.29
2009	2.41	3.20	3.71	1.06	1.35
2010-2013	0.36	0.08	0.35	0.91	0.84
Total	0.70	0.64	1.08	0.18	0.71

Source: Bloomberg

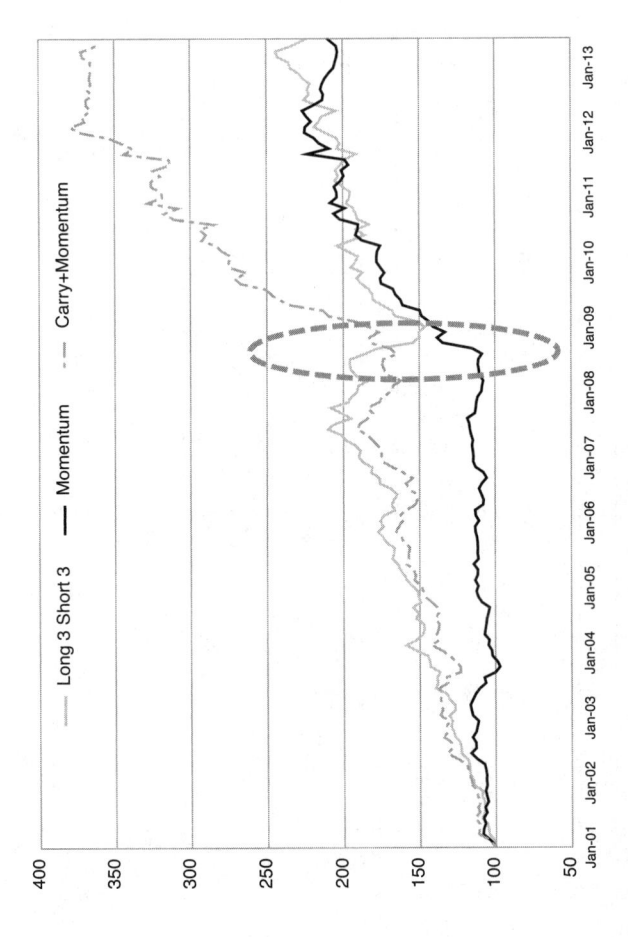

Figure 2-11 Momentum as a hedge to carry

Some Remarks

In an unprecedented environment of record low interest rates, where the Federal Reserve signals a low rate until at least 2014 and with other major economies following suit, a carry strategy remains an attractive investment for investors starved for yields. This chapter discussed how to elevate and improve the simplest individual currency carry trade through diversification, VIX filtering, and hedging with a momentum strategy.

What has been presented so far is only the most basic illustration of building a rule based strategy. There are myriad ways to improve results by employing additional rules and filters, such as using the carry risk ratio, purchasing power parity, and changes in yield.[7]

Will VIX filtering really aid you in the next crisis as it would have in the past? The truth is that no one knows. It is possible the next crisis could be so unique and unprecedented that it rewrites economics, but it isn't likely. It is possible we may discover a new subatomic particle that rewrites physics, but that shouldn't impede us from teaching and applying the standard model. There is more evidence on the side of history and academic research that VIX filtering should work than there is to the contrary. What is certain is that the market is constantly evolving, and rules and strategies must adapt along with it.

---

[7] Ang, Andrew and Joseph S. Chen. "Yield Curve Predictors of Foreign Exchange Returns." Working Paper, 2010.

3

Rule Based Value Investment

Value in Emerging Markets

Value investing typically refers to the process of selecting single name stocks. Investors employ a variety of methods to determine and analyze a company's true "value" using factors such as book value, price-to-earnings and book-to-market ratio. Starting with Fama and French[1] numerous ratios have been derived to help investors in screening and selecting the best stocks to go long or short. Although value investing isn't typically thought of as a rule based system, in truth it is because the guidelines and criteria of value investing are a series of rules and filters used to separate the mediocre stocks from the valuable. Rather than invest in a company because it's become popular or because of a charismatic CEO, or because of recent success, the rules of value investing strip away the emotion and focus on the economic foundations of a company. Many books and academic papers are in circulation on value investing in equities, so let's instead turn our attention to expanding the principles and framework of value investing to an asset class with enormous potential that is increasingly vital for diversification: emerging markets (EM).

---

[1] Fama, Eugene F. and Kenneth R. French. "Dividend Yields and Expected Stock Returns." *Journal of Financial Economics* 22 (October 1988): 3–25.

Emerging markets have generated enormous interest over the past decade with buzzwords like *BRICS* (Brazil, Russia, India, China, and South Africa) becoming ubiquitous. Emerging markets seemingly promise exotic returns from places in the world with growth rates G10 nations can only envy. A shrewd investor has every reason to be cautious; it is difficult to discern the hype from the reality. A typical investment platitude is "invest in what you know," and with a handful of companies that might be possible to some extent, but it would shut out opportunities in emerging markets. After all, how can an individual investor hope to truly understand the Brazilian economy without reading or speaking Portuguese? At the same time a total aversion to emerging markets is not an option for the intelligent investor as it sacrifices diversification. Particularly in the wake of the 2008 crisis, emerging markets were more resilient than G10 economies, and a globally diversified portfolio would have benefitted greatly.

The growth of emerging markets is an easily recognized source of persistent returns. Demographics are destiny: Where there is population growth, abundant natural resources, low labor costs, and an improving quality of life, the economic potential is enormous. At the same time, most developed economies, with the notable exception of the United States, face the problem of a gentrifying population and falling birth rates, trends with grave consequences for the future. Emerging markets nations are at a starkly different point in history than they were at the end of the twentieth century. With greater political stability, economies that had lain fallow for decades are modernizing at incredible speed. As the middle class grows in nations as diverse as China, India, and Brazil, not only does domestic demand thrive with millions of new consumers purchasing their first cars and appliances, the demand also grows for competent institutions, reduced corruption, and improved infrastructure. A virtuous cycle of positive reinforcement results in exciting GDP growth and other fundamental metrics.

As well as demographics, modern technology acts as a catalyst in spurring growth in emerging markets. Through the Internet and greater connectivity, information is democratized, and ideas spread faster than they ever have. A farmer in rural Brazil can check the weather and make electronic payments through a cell phone with a solar charger. A villager in India can access a microloan from across the world to start a business. The Internet offers millions access to the world's libraries and information at the touch of a button. Social media further serves to unite the like-minded, to expose public abuses, and to organize protests and demonstrations. Borders are increasingly obsolete, and talent, no matter from where it originates, can rise to the top of an equally level playing field. In emerging markets the population is ever greater, with a higher quality of life and greater access to education and free information than has ever been possible. It is worth realizing that the stage is set, and the world is poised for a blossoming of human genius unrivaled in world history, and only a true global portfolio can hope to capture the returns.

Where there is opportunity however, there is almost certainly danger, and emerging markets are no exception. Emerging markets' returns experience a greater skewness and kurtosis than developed market returns. What this means is that when a crisis occurs and markets go down, they do so in a particularly dramatic fashion for emerging markets. On the other hand in the aftermath of the crisis, emerging markets recovered more robustly than G10 economies. These are only some of the dangers involved with sovereign governments that are young and maturing; political winds are fickle, and economic gains are no guarantee against revolt in nations with a populace scarred by deep fault lines of inequality. Gradual progressive changes might not be occurring fast enough for people struggling to survive, and there are numerous historical examples of nations that have nationalized industries and defaulted on external debt. Furthermore, a significant challenge of investing in emerging markets is that each nation has a unique and complex character, culture, and historical narrative.

How do we filter such an overwhelming sea of information into deciding whether or not to invest in a country? Complicating matters further is that there is often a scarcity of reliable up-to-date information for some emerging market countries. If thoroughly analyzing an entire country is a daunting task for any individual investor, analyzing a basket of countries is next to impossible. Expertise and endless hours of geo-political research are not an efficient approach to achieving truly global diversification. What is needed is a framework of rules to automate the decision-making process to take into account both the historical "fundamentals" of a country, as well as gauging the level of uncertainty in the credit default swap markets.

The greater goal of investing in emerging markets, as well as the magnitude and stability of the investment returns themselves, is the diversification this asset class brings to any portfolio. The economic fate of unique and disparate countries shows little correlation to G10 economies or to each other. During a major crisis all risky assets are highly correlated, and emerging markets are no different, although they tend to recover faster in the wake of the crisis. The same obstacles that made emerging market countries so opaque to analysis produce a unique and vibrant source of diversification. The value of diversification cannot be emphasized enough because the scientific truth is that diversification is the rock upon which profitable stable investing is based.

Emerging markets have gone from a niche frontier investment to an asset class of increasingly growing importance, vital to portfolio diversification and profitability. How do we now go from a strong interest in emerging markets to placing an actual investment? By default many assume the local stock exchange would be a sensible place to start, but arguably, bonds and currency are historically superior alternatives. In this chapter you apply a basic "value" analysis on fundamental, macro-economic data that helps reveal how investing in emerging markets is largely about the "value of the country."

A "value" investing style is well-suited to the unique characteristics of emerging markets. Monetary interventions are typically more frequent for emerging market countries; when intervention occurs, market reacts in an abrupt fashion. There are strategies that depend solely on historical price patterns that are successful. In the previous chapter you learned about the momentum strategy, which relies on historical data as an indicator of future success. Momentum is of limited use in this situation because it does not take into account of the impact of monetary intervention to the market prices. Another concern is that liquidity can be limited in emerging markets. When liquidity is limited, as every trader is well aware, the prices on the screens become unreliable, the bid/ask spreads widen, and exiting a position can come at a steep cost. For these reasons strategies based purely on technical indicators are not the best fit for investment in EM.

Instead of using historical price data, simple rules based on macroeconomic fundamentals are applied to both currencies and hard currency denominated sovereign bonds, the two more liquid instruments in emerging markets. The analysis in this chapter looks at each country's growth, inflation, debt level, and interest rates to select good carry and credit worthiness. This strategy takes the backward-looking information of economic performance into account as a basic filter to help you determine which countries to invest in. The historical data is complemented by forward-looking indicators, improving the fundamental-based strategy by taking into account the market sentiment expressed in the credit default swap market. The analysis factors in both fundamental data as well as the live market expectation of each country's ability to service its debt.

Credit default swaps (CDS) can be thought of as simply insurance policies for bond holders. Suppose an investor holds an extensive portfolio of illiquid bonds for an emerging market country yielding 6% and there is political event, such as an election, that creates temporary uncertainty. Rather than incur the expense of liquidating the portfolio, it is more efficient to buy one-year or two-year protection. For greater peace of mind, the investor is willing to buy the protection by paying a premium of 2% to keep the principal safe in the event of default over the next one or two years—this means that the premium, often called "spread", of a credit default swap can be viewed as a live risk indicator for a specific credit market.[2]

It is worth noting that credit default swaps have received a bad reputation since the subprime crises in 2007/2008 and the European/Greek crises in 2010. Credit default swaps are contracts, and the fine legal print of what does and does not constitute a "default" is difficult for even corporate lawyers to understand, much less so for individual investors. The collapse of Bear Stearns in 2008 for instance, did not trigger a "credit event" as their bonds continued to be serviced by J.P. Morgan. When Lehman Brothers fell a few months after, a credit event was triggered with low recovery of principal (~7%). AIG, which was also in crisis during late 2008, did trigger a credit event; however, due to intervention by the U.S. Government, recovery of principal was high. Arbitrary factors heavily influenced these results, which complicates efforts to invest systematically.

Assuming you held a basket of CDS that involved these three contracts, there would have been three different outcomes. These inconsistent results after crisis events create too many unknowns, and for this reason and others, it is not recommended for individuals to invest in the CDS market. This is merely to recognize that CDS markets react to the same fundamentals as the underlying bonds, and often for an emerging country, the CDS market reacts faster than the bond market. You can take advantage of the information CDS market prices offer, serving as a legitimate and real-time market barometer for the credit worthiness of a specific country.

---

[2] For an excellent, updated description of CDS, please see Tuckman and Serrat's *Fixed Income Securities Tools for Today's Markets*, 2011, Chapter 19. (Listed in the Bibliography.)

Value Investing in Emerging Market FX

Outside of equities such as in the foreign exchange and bond markets, "value" no longer has a straight-forward definition. The true value of a bond, for instance, in literal terms means its future real bond yield, or rather bond yield minus inflation. This value of course depends on the credit risk of the bond and inflation. In foreign exchange, value often means the "fair value" given by purchasing power parity.[3] "Value investing" here means that it is possible to subject emerging market countries to an analysis similar to that used in "value investing" for stocks, only instead of choosing companies that are fundamentally undervalued, you use the rules to select countries that have the greatest fundamental potential for currency appreciation and bond returns. Let's look at how to create and apply these filters over the coming sections.

Investors seek out emerging economies due to their high growth rates; however, there is the important matter of how to best access this growth. Conventional wisdom would tell us it is through the stock market. In the U.S. when politicians praise the economy, they don't mention exchange rates or bonds markets, but rather where the Dow Jones Industrial Average closes. In a developed market it is true that corporate earnings should grow inline with the economy. Emerging markets are another story, however, and high economic growth is not necessarily coupled to a strong domestic stock market. There is lack of statistical evidence that stock returns of emerging economies and their GDP growth are correlated at all. Henry and Kanmann analyzed 30 years of data and concluded that "not only is the relationship between stock returns and economic growth statistically insignificant,

---

[3] Simply speaking, purchasing power parity rate, or PPP rate, is the exchange rate that equates the amount of money needed to purchase the same goods and services in two countries. For example, the Big Mac Index published by *The Economist* is the implicit exchange rates with which a Big Mac would cost the same in every country.

the sign of the relationship actually goes the wrong way." There is weak evidence the opposite relationship may be true.[4]

Another analysis by Ritter that studied 19 major countries between 1900 and 2011 shows the correlaltion is -0.39.[5] One plausible explanation of this unintuitive result is that stock returns are determined by earning growth per share, not economy-wide corporate earning growth.[5]

Currency appreciation is a superior alternative that is strongly correlated with growth: As a country grows, it attracts an influx of capital. Figure 3-1 shows the correlations between currency appreciation and GDP growth of 31 emerging countries between 2001 to 2010.[6] The correlation between emerging market GDP growth and currency appreciation is 21% on the average, whereas the correlation with EM equity indices is -6%. Investing in EM growth via EM currencies is also favorable due to improving FX liquidity. The 2010 Bank of International Settlements (BIS) Triennial Central Bank survey showed rapid grow in the turnover in EM currencies, with daily volume of $879 billion, a 210% increase from 2001 to 2010. Offshore trading, meaning foreign exchange traded outside a currency's home country, has grown particulary fast, such as approximately 22 billion for the Chinese Renmibi and 17 billion for the Indian Rupee in Singapore per day.

---

[4] Henry and Kannan (2008) includes data from Argentina, Brazil, Chile, China, Colombia, India, Indonesia, Jordan, Korea, Malaysia, Mexico, Nigeria, Pakistan, Philippines, South Africa, Thailand, Turkey, Venezuela, and Zimbabwe. They regressed stock returns on the growth with resulting coefficient of -0.62 with a t-statistics of 0.7.

[5] Ritter, Jay. "Is Economic Growth Good for Investors?" *Journal of Applied Corporate Finance* 24(3) (Summer 2012): 8–18.

[6] Data kindly provided by Credit Suisse.

CHAPTER 3 • RULE BASED VALUE INVESTMENT **117**

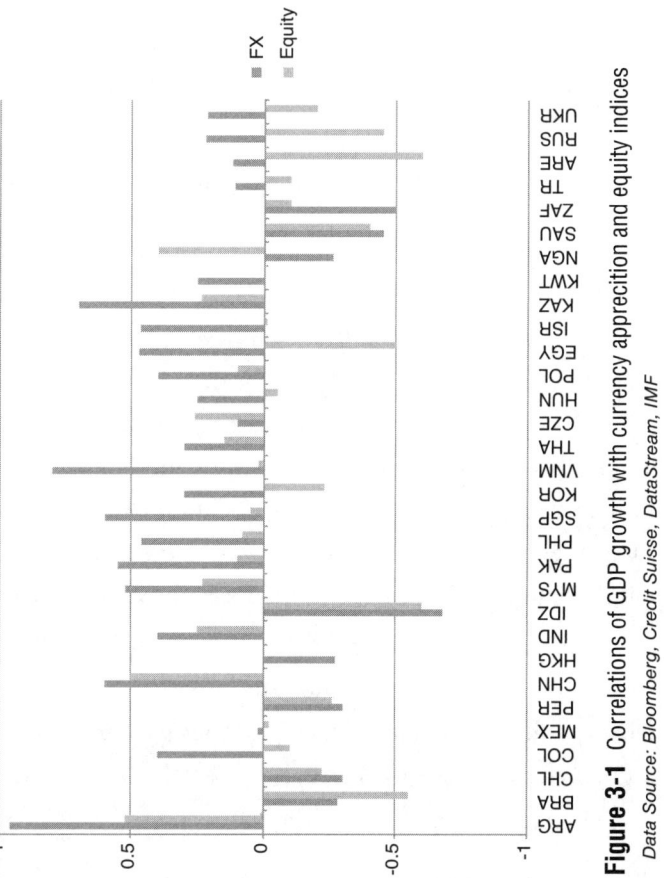

Figure 3-1 Correlations of GDP growth with currency apprecition and equity indices
Data Source: Bloomberg, Credit Suisse, DataStream, IMF

For some time academic research has documented positive returns of carry trades in emerging market currencies.[7] It has been observed that although macro-economic/fundamental variables help to forecast exchange rates over the long term, short-term movement is better predicted by technical rules. In developing a rule based investment for EM FX, the first step is to construct a "value" filter based on economic fundamentals. To complement this strategy that draws on historical data, forward-looking information from credit default swap market will be incorporated to further strengthen the result.

Rule Based Investment in Emerging Market FX

Constructing and implementing a rule based strategy in emerging markets foreign exchange is the next task. For the purposes here, let's select the following 10 countries to invest against the U.S. Dollar: Brazil, Hungary, Indonesia, Malaysia, Mexico, Poland, Russia, South Africa, Thailand, and Turkey. There are other EM currencies investors should also consider due to their improving liquidity, economic condition, and possible benefit of diversification from a larger portfolio, such as Chile, China, the Czech Republic, India, Kuwait, Nigeria, Philippines, Saudi Arabia, Singapore, South Korea, and Taiwan.

Analogous to the carry strategies in Chapter 2, "Rule Based Carry and Momentum Investment," the monthly investment rule is to buy fixed dollar amounts of emerging country currencies via one-month currency forwards. The return of each currency will be the

---

[7] Recent studies are, among others, Bansal and Dahlquist (2000), Frankel and Poonawala (2006), Burnside, Eichenbaum and Rebelo (2007), de Zwart, Markwat, Swinkels and van Dijk (2008), Ranaldo and Söderlind (2010), Lustig, Roussanov and Verdelhan (2011).

spot appreciation plus the interest rate differential between the EM currencies and U.S. dollar. Many emerging market currencies don't have a tradable forward market due to capital control and convertibility issues. Or, there might exist a tradable forward market, but only available to onshore investors. Among others, Brazil, Indonesia, Malaysia, and Thailand are good examples. For these currencies, non-deliverable forward markets (NDF) have been developed and are traded offshore. The major difference between deliverable and NDF market is that the latter is settled in cash, that is, no physical delivery takes place.

Return characteristics of emerging market currencies selected in this investment universe are reported in Table 3-1. It should not come as a surprise that compared with G10 currencies, EM currencies delivered on average close to double the returns of G10 currencies over the period between January 2001 and June 2013. It should also be expected that they are more negatively skewed and have a larger kurtosis than G10 currencies. In other words, EM currencies have had a greater frequency of negative returns and extreme movement than G10 currencies. EM currencies are more profitable than G10 currencies, but they are also more volatile, yet the Sharpe ratio indicates the rewards exceed the additional risk. Figure 3-2 illustrates the risk adjusted cumulative returns of the EM currency carries relative to the average of G10 currencies. The Sharpe ratio for G10 currency returns is 0.31 and that of EM currency returns is 1.83, signaling a superior risk-adjusted investment.

Table 3-1 Performance Statistics of Individual Emerging Market Currency Carry Against U.S. $ (January 2001–June 2013)

	BRL	HUF	IDR	MXN	MYR	PLZ	RUB	THB	TRY	ZAR	EM Average	G10 Average
Annualized Avg. Return in %	10.82	8.72	9.01	3.19	1.96	6.70	4.55	4.82	12.43	6.17	6.84	3.50
Annualized Return Standard Deviation in %	18.09	15.48	12.42	10.24	6.43	14.77	9.67	5.83	18.25	17.96	12.91	11.30
Monthly Return Skewness	-0.77	-0.97	1.31	-1.18	-0.38	-0.80	-1.60	-0.16	-1.37	-0.43	-0.63	-0.34
Monthly Return Kurtosis	2.94	2.57	9.35	5.28	2.03	1.58	8.78	0.47	8.11	0.14	4.12	1.36
Max. One Month Loss in %	-19.45	-17.67	-12.99	-14.38	-6.85	-14.41	-14.63	-4.36	-29.50	-14.67	-14.89	-11.20
Sharpe Ratio	2.07	1.95	2.51	1.08	1.06	1.57	1.63	2.87	2.36	1.19	1.83	0.31

Source: Bloomberg

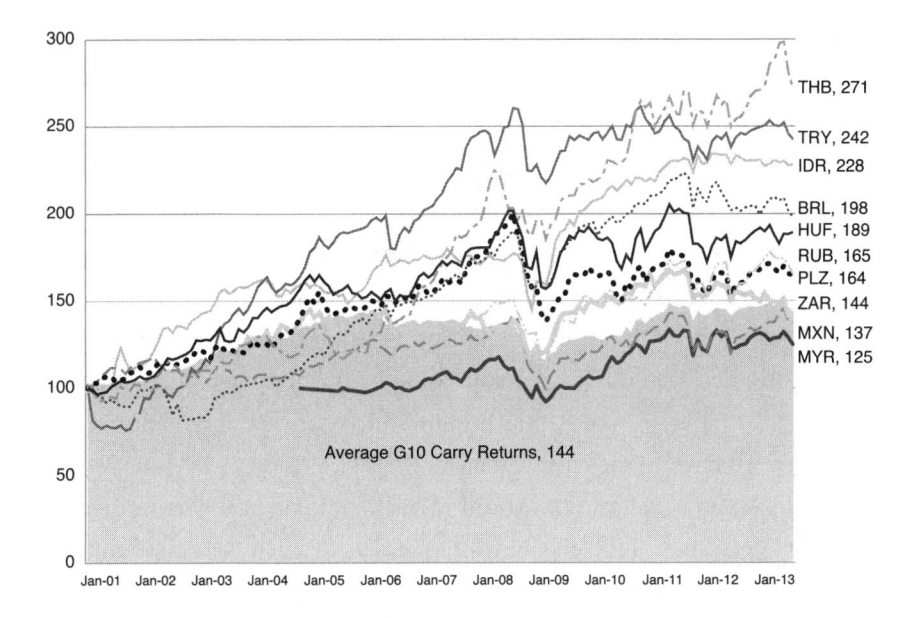

Figure 3-2 Risk-adjusted cumulative carry returns (volatility = 10%)

Fundamental Rules

Determining the intrinsic value of a currency can be done in many ways. They range from the simple Big Mac index published by *The Economist* every month (which uses just one variable, the price of a Big Mac in different countries around the world) to complex econometric models using multiple factors such as a country's growth, inflation, foreign reserve, openness of the economy, health of the banking system, and so on. This portion of the chapter focuses on three key macro-economic variables of an economy: growth, inflation, and the level of short-term interest rates. Rather than build a statistical model, let's simply employ a basic ranking system.

Each country is ranked according to its GDP growth, inflation, and short-term interest rates (again using Brazil, Hungary, Indonesia, Malaysia, Mexico, Poland, Russia, South Africa, Thailand, and

Turkey). High GDP growth is desirable as strong economies produce strong currencies. Inflation is certainly a critical concern as it degrades the value of a currency. High inflation is a major red flag that often threatens social unrest. With short-term interest rates, the higher the better because this is where "carry" return comes from. If short-term interest rates are too low, there is little potential profit. On a monthly basis you can rank EM countries by GDP growth, inflation, and interest rates and only buy the "upper half" of the countries at the top of the list. You don't "go short" or sell any currencies that rank in the bottom. The reason is that the emerging market currencies studied here all have higher interest rates than U.S. Dollar. If you were to short these currencies, you would incur negative carry, meaning you would have pay to hold that position, which is costly. In other words, the expected return of selling short has to be higher than the carry in order to be profitable.

More sophisticated rules are required to confidently go both long and short the risk premium. The investment philosophy throughout this book has been that if the market is agitated and there is no smart risk to take, it is the best to close out the trade and park your capital into the money market. As tempting as it is to want to profit from going both long and short carry, remember that this is analogous to transitioning between being an insurance company and insurance policy holder. As an insurance company, the premium received must always outweigh the risks covered in the long term to ensure long-term profitability. As an insurance policy holder, it is overwhelmingly likely that you will pay out more than you will collect. Unless there is a crisis. Crisis events are however relatively few and far between; going short carry in the hopes of a big profit in a crisis is typically a losing strategy of paying the "insurance premium" to someone else.

Do not treat buying and selling insurance as equal transactions because they aren't; there will always exist a market bias toward insurance companies/sellers. Natural market demand for protection determines a price of protection that on average in the long term must outweigh the actual risk of losses. It's better only to play the role of the insurance company and stand aside, taking off risk during volatile periods.

The fundamental metrics used to rank our list of EM countries consists of backward-looking information because GDP growth and inflation data are not available in real time. This economic data is often only available to the public after a delay and is often subject to adjustments in subsequent months. Therefore, to be on the conservative side, use GDP growth and inflation numbers from six months prior to determine the investment for the upcoming month. For short-term rates, it is the rate of the previous month used in the study.

The fundamental rule based strategy is implemented through ranking: Each month, you can rank all 10 EM countries into three lists according to their GDP growth, inflation, and short-term rates. You buy and hold those currencies (against USD) for the top-five ranked countries through one-month forwards. Each currency has an equal dollar amount invested at the beginning of the month. These strategies will be referred to as GDP growth, inflation, and interest rates strategies, respectively. This means you buy and hold the currencies of the top five countries with the highest GDP growth, the top five countries with the lowest inflation, and the top five countries with the highest short-terms rates. Investors are, of course, subject to different transaction costs, so let's assume a conservative cost of 1.2% per year (10 basis points per month) to maintain each strategy.

Using data from January 2001 to June 2013, the results of the three fundamental strategies based on ranking are recorded in Table 3-2. All three fundamental strategies outperform an equally weighted simple buy-and-hold portfolio. The short rate strategy delivered the highest return of an annualized 9.3%, outperforming the equally weighted portfolio by over 3%. The return of the short rate strategy, however, also has the highest volatility of 11%, which is 1.7% higher than the simple equally weighted portfolio. Risk-adjusted returns are similar among three macro strategies, ranging from 0.8 to 0.86.

Table 3-2 Performance Statistics of Fundamental Ranking Rules for EM Currency Investment (January 2001–June 2013)

	Average Annualized Return in %				Annualized Standard Deviation of Return in %				Sharpe Ratio			
	Eq. Weight	GDP	Inflation	Short Rates	Eq. Weight	GDP	Inflation	Short Rates	Eq. Weight	GDP	Inflation	Short Rates
2001-2007	9.07	10.18	15.17	13.89	6.54	7.43	8.02	8.45	1.39	1.37	1.89	1.64
2008	-10.60	-7.30	-11.50	-8.81	14.37	13.03	16.34	17.40	-0.74	-0.56	-0.70	-0.51
2009	16.24	20.94	21.32	25.15	12.32	13.19	12.22	12.81	1.32	1.59	1.75	1.96
2010-2013	-2.52	-0.64	-3.83	-3.01	10.37	9.28	11.74	11.92	-0.24	-0.07	-0.33	-0.25
Total	5.78	7.48	9.17	9.34	9.25	9.34	10.61	11.03	0.62	0.80	0.86	0.85

Source: Bloomberg, DataStream, IMF

The three fundamental based strategies can be combined together by averaging the three macro rankings. As before, on a monthly basis buy only those currencies against the USD whose joint macro signals are ranked in the top five. The results are reported in Table 3-3. Our ranking-based macro strategy achieves an annualized net return of 10% over the period 2001 to 2013, outperforming the simple equally weighted EM currency portfolio. This strategy greatly outperforms the S&P 500, which obtained an annualized return of 2.8% over the same period. On the risk front, the macro strategy has slightly higher overall volatility than the equally weighted portfolio discussed earlier, but the returns exceed the additional risk taken. Ranking-based macro strategy achieves a Sharpe of 1.0, outperforming the equally weighted EM currency portfolio and the S&P 500.

Table 3-3 Performance Statistics of Combined Fundamental Ranking Rules for EM Currency Investment (January 2001–June 2013)

	Average Annualized Return in %		Annualized Standard Deviation of Return in %		Sharpe Ratio	
	Ten Currencies Eq. Weight	Macro	Ten Currencies Eq. Weight	Macro	Ten Currencies Eq. Weight	Macro
2001-2007	9.07	14.72	6.54	8.08	1.39	1.82
2008	-10.60	-10.99	14.37	16.10	-0.74	-0.68
2009	16.24	28.30	12.32	13.70	1.32	2.07
2010-2013	-2.52	-0.04	7.84	10.40	-0.24	0.00
Total	5.78	10.00	9.25	10.39	0.62	0.96

Source: Bloomberg, DataStream, IMF

Many professional investors use more sophisticated versions of fundamental models to determine the fair value of exchange rates. Readers who are interested in refining the fundamental strategy are encouraged to investigate other macro-economic variables. It is also possible that instead of going only long, to expand the strategy to a

USD neutral, that is, both long and short, by buying, for example, top-five currencies and shorting bottom-five currencies according to their rankings. But be aware of the cost of negative carry. In constructing a portfolio, instead of equally weighting every country, meaning each is allocated an equal amount of funds, it is better to employ inverse volatility weighting to further improve the Sharpe ratio. With inverse volatility weighting, the lower the volatility of a country, the greater the capital allocation it receives, and the higher the volatility, the lower the capital allocation. The results of this process are to reduce the variance of the final sum.

Let's review the rule based EM portfolio so far: Focusing on currency, it's gone from the "simplest case" of a naïve equally weighted basket toward three slightly more sophisticated strategies of ranking based on the macro-economic factors of GDP, inflation, and short-term rates, to finally combining the three strategies into a single macro/fundamental strategy producing greater returns with a superior Sharpe ratio as well. Don't be too comfortable with this strategy alone because the data used is from six months ago, and the world changes quickly. As well as looking backward, let's look ahead and check market sentiment through CDS prices.

Technical Rules: Overlaying Credit Default Swap Spread as Market Indicator

Previous chapters have described the use of the VIX extensively as the "fear barometer" to read the market's anticipation of upcoming crises. In this chapter let's look at another risk indicator particularly relevant for investing in individual emerging countries: Sovereign Credit Default Swap (SCDS is simply CDS for a sovereign country; CDS and SCDS are used here interchangeably). SCDS, as has been discussed previously, offers protection against the credit risk of a country's sovereign bonds—it is an insurance for bond holders afraid of a default. Generally speaking, market makers, so-called "sell side," are the principal buyers and sellers of CDS to hedge their portfolios and illiquid risk. Hedge funds and mutual funds, so-called "buy side," use short CDS positions to go long a credit mainly because of the superior funding terms (like buying a bond on margin), and they use long CDS positions to avoid the hassles of selling a bond. Typically to buy a $5 million bond requires $5 million. However, through CDS it is possible to gain exposure to the credit risk of the bond without having to fund the bond purchase. To sell a bond, on the other hand, requires first borrowing it through a repurchase agreement, so-called "repo," which can become expensive for certain bonds.

Sovereign CDS spreads can be used to read the market's expectation of the credit worthiness of a country. It can be incorporated in an investment strategy in a straight-forward fashion: If one country's CDS spread deteriorates dramatically over the previous month, you avoid investing in that country's currency in the upcoming month. For the purpose of this exercise, an increase in CDS spreads of more than 20% are defined as "dramatic" (this is an arbitrary value not derived from data mining but for illustrative purposes only). For example, for June 2013, you would have avoided investing in Brazil and South Africa because the CDS spreads of these two countries had risen more than 20% from end of April to end of May. In November 2008, you would have stayed out of all 10 emerging market currencies because for all 10 countries considered here, their CDS spreads had widened more than 20%. Figure 3-3 illustrates the dramatic increase of emerging sovereign CDS spreads during the 2008 Financial Crisis.

In short, a sovereign CDS spread serves as a risk indicator for each individual EM country, as opposed to VIX, which serves as a general risk indicator for the global financial markets. Instead of using one single barometer, it's important to recognize that each country has its own political/financial crises. However, when the CDS spread of all countries rises dramatically, it is a powerful message from the credit market that global market deterioration is anticipated.

128 Rule Based Investing

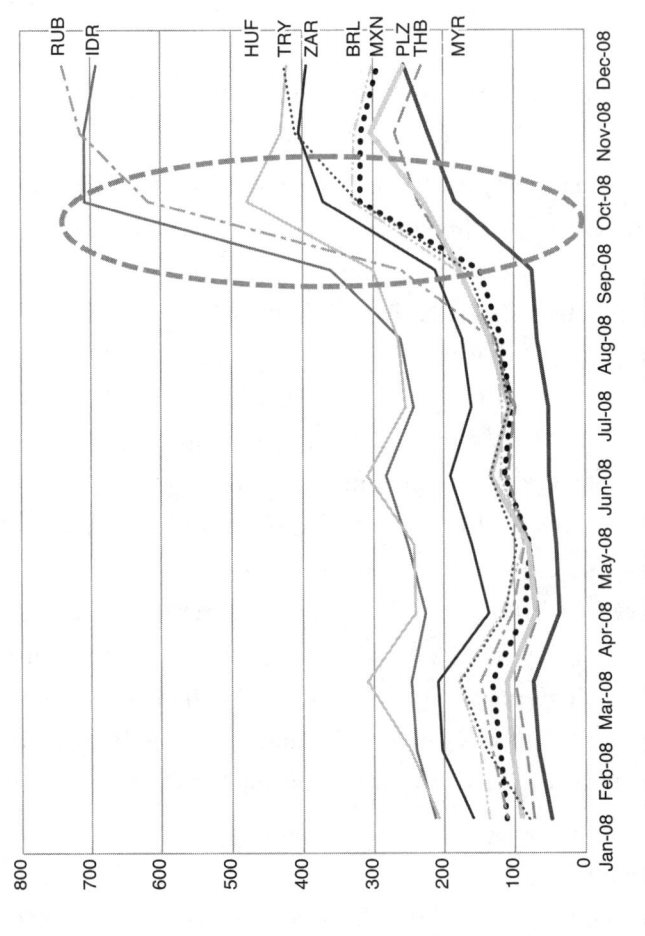

Figure 3-3 Sovereign credit default swap spreads in 2008

The results of applying the sovereign CDS spread filter to the EM currency investments are reported in Table 3-4. The CDS filtering rule achieves a higher return (9.8% per annum) compared to an equally weighted portfolio and comparable with the fundamental/macro strategy. It also impressively reduces overall volatility. Notably, maximal one-month loss is much lower than that from a macro strategy (7% versus 12.2%). In 2008, while the macro/fundamental filters failed to reduce volatility or maximal loss compared with an equally weighted portfolio, the CDS filter helps to cut maximal one-month loss by half. And it achieves an overall Sharpe ratio of 1.24.

Table 3-4 Performance Statistics of CDS Filtering Strategy for EM Currency Investment (January 2001–June 2013)

	Average Annualized Return in %		Annualized Standard Deviation of Return in %		Sharpe Ratio	
	Ten Currencies Eq. Weight	*CDS Filter*	*Ten Currencies Eq. Weight*	*CDS Filter*	*Ten Currencies Eq. Weight*	*CDS Filter*
2001-2007	9.07	11.77	6.54	6.17	1.39	1.91
2008	-10.60	1.08	14.37	9.42	-0.74	0.11
2009	16.24	17.72	12.32	12.19	1.32	1.45
2010-2013	-2.52	5.13	7.84	8.58	-0.32	0.60
Total	5.78	9.76	9.34	7.86	0.62	1.24

Source: Bloomberg, DataStream, IMF

So far we have built two separate strategies: a macro/fundamental ranking strategy and a risk indicator filtering strategy. The use of simple fundamental macro ranking tables produced superior results than simply buying and holding a basket of countries. CDS filtering complements this strategy with forward-looking components derived from real-time market sentiment.

In evaluating the forward-looking rules and fundamental rules side-by-side, in this situation the forward-looking CDS filter produced superior risk-adjusted results than the fundamental ranking filter. Use of the CDS filter on its own produces smarter investment returns than both the simple strategy and macro ranking strategy can produce. When the CDS filter is compared to the macro ranking strategy, the return is similar, but the Sharpe ratio is superior for the CDS filtering. As before, the best results are achieved by combining the backward- and forward-looking strategies into a greater whole.

Combining Fundamental Rules and Risk Indicators

Let's now combine a macro based ranking system with the sovereign CDS spread filter. The combined strategy is implemented in a straight-forward fashion: Each month, you select the top five countries from the macro/fundamental ranking system. If any of these five countries' CDS spreads have risen more than 20% over the past month, you don't invest in its currency in the upcoming month. The capital is reallocated to the remaining currencies. If none of the countries passes the CDS filter, you allocate the capital to U.S. money markets for that month.

As shown in Table 3-5, this macro/technical rule combined EM currency strategy achieved an annualized return of 14.3% from January 2001 to June 2013, net of transaction cost. It outperforms the simple equally weighted EM currency portfolio, the rule based macro strategy, and the stand-alone CDS strategy in overall return as well as on a risk adjusted basis. Sharpe ratio is 1.57, more than double that of the equally weighted portfolio (0.62).

Let's pause and reflect on these results and their implications. So far the strategy has been to take a simple methodology and ranking table any economics undergraduate should be capable of constructing, and combine it with the filtering power of CDS spread. It is remarkable that such a basic exercise achieves such improved results. Whereas the S&P 500 annually returned 2.8% from January 2001 to June 2013, the combined strategy generated a 14.3% return, and the Sharpe ratio improved from 0.18 to 1.57, respectively. This rule has not been artificially selected for deceptively high returns; the truth is that simple principles have profound effects. Figure 3-4 illustrates the risk adjusted cumulative returns of the rule based strategies compared with the simple equally weighted portfolio and S&P 500.

To invest in emerging markets, rather than pursuing a long process of gaining expertise, it is more efficient to instead use a framework of rules. Rather than just randomly selecting an assortment of emerging market countries, you can construct tables that rank countries by fundamental macro-economic value and select the best countries. If we had to select a basketball team from a field of dozens of players, it makes intuitive sense that rather than picking names out of a hat, ranking players by their statistics and choosing the top five will produce superior results. Who would bet on the random team against the ranked team?

You can then further improve the results by checking real-time market sentiment before investing. The fundamental based ranking strategies rely on data from six months prior; CDS prices, however, are a live reflection of what the market is currently charging for "credit insurance." A country may seem to have sound economic fundamentals, but if CDS spreads are widening for that country, it means something is causing the "insurance rate" to rise. It is safer to avoid that trade for the month.

What should be very exciting is that this example is only the simplest case model. The return of 14.3% is already high, and the potential for improvement is vast.

Table 3-5 Performance Statistics of Fundamental Combined with CDS Filtering Strategy for EM Currency Investment (January 2001–June 2013)

	Average Annualized Return in %		Annualized Standard Deviation of Return in %		Sharpe Ratio	
	Ten Currencies Eq. Weight	*Combined Rules*	*Ten Currencies Eq. Weight*	*Combined Rules*	*Ten Currencies Eq. Weight*	*Combined Rules*
2001-2007	9.07	18.76	6.54	7.05	1.39	2.66
2008	-10.60	4.58	14.37	10.32	-0.74	0.44
2009	16.24	28.52	12.32	13.66	1.32	2.09
2010-2013	-2.52	3.35	7.84	9.88	-0.32	0.34
Total	5.78	14.30	9.34	9.10	0.62	1.57

Source: Bloomberg, DataStream, IMF

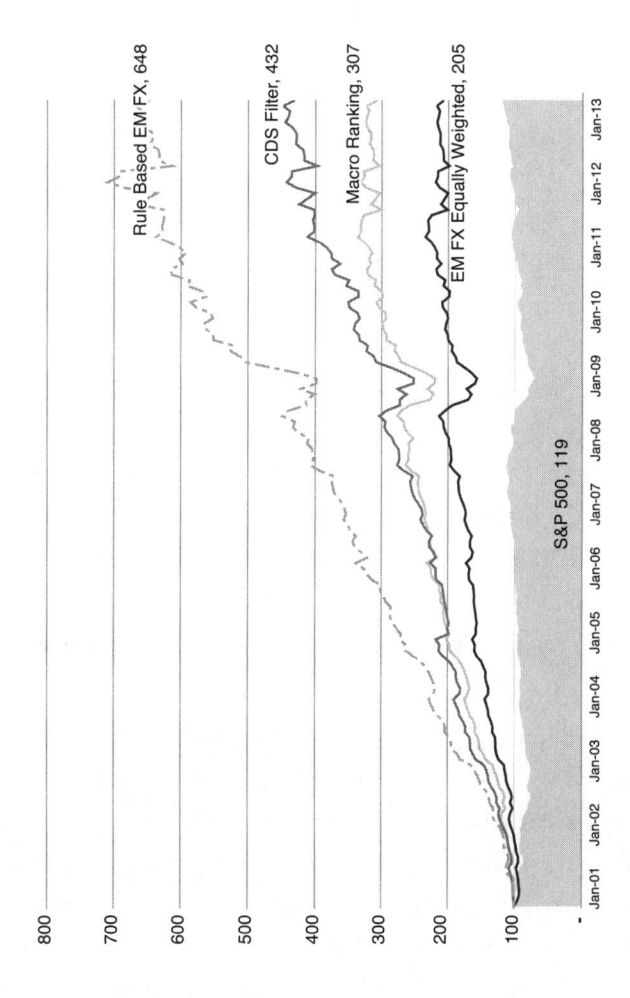

Figure 3-4 Risk-adjusted cumulative returns (volatility = 10%)

Value Investing in Emerging Market Sovereign Bonds

A diversified EM portfolio must reflect more than only currencies. The efforts here with EM currency have produced a strategy with returns of 14.3% and a Sharpe ratio of 1.6. Now let's similarly examine and construct rules for U.S. Dollar denominated EM bonds.

There are two types of debts issued by sovereigns of emerging markets: local currency denominated and hard currency denominated. Although both types of debts are subject to their particular sovereign credit risk, the returns of local currency denominated debt are subject to additional currency risk for USD-based investors and are inherently more volatile. For example, bonds issued by Brazil can be denominated in the Brazilian Real or in the U.S. Dollar. If the Real appreciates against the Dollar, then a dollar-based investor's return is the bond return plus the currency gain. Risk factors other than exchange rates that impact local currency denominated bonds are, for example, local interest rates. Also there is the legal risk of different jurisdictions; that is, local bonds are subject to local laws, whereas hard currency bonds are subject to international law. In this chapter only investments in hard currency dominated bonds are considered.

Analogous to selecting single stocks, there is a vast body of academic research dedicated to a country's credit risk and the return of its bonds. According to Reinhart and Rogoff, five factors determine if a country is in crisis and headed toward default: the amount of external and domestic government debt, inflation outbursts, currency crashes, and banking crises.[8] Baek, Bandopadhyaya, and Du found a significant impact to specific macro-economic variables such as inflation, GDP growth, foreign reserve, real exchange rates, in crisis scenarios.[9]

---

[8] Reinhart, Carmen and Kenneth Rogoff. *This Time Is Different: Eight Centuries of Financial Folly*. Brew Herset: Princeton University Press, 2008.

[9] Baek, In-Mee, Arindam Bandopadhyaya, and Chan Du. "Determinants of Market-Assessed Sovereign Risk: Economic Fundamentals or Market Risk Appetite?" *Journal of International Money and Finance* 24 (June 2005) 533–548.

Their work also studies the impact of a risk appetite index derived from stock returns and volatilities. To summarize, those factors that measure a country's ability to service its debt such as its growth, debt to GDP ratio, inflation, reserve, current account, real exchange rates are the salient risk factors of an emerging market bond's return.

As with the rule based strategies built for EM currencies earlier, instead of building and estimating a multi-factor statistical model for EM bond returns, let's consider a simple ranking strategy to determine which country's bonds are worth investing in, focusing on the macro/fundamental ranking first and then complement those returns with the forward-looking component of a sovereign CDS spread filter.

For the purposes of comparison, these investment rules for bonds are the same as the one for FX, investing on a monthly basis and each month selecting the top five countries to buy hard currency denominated government debt according to their macro-economic condition via a simple ranking system. The transaction cost for EM bonds are on average higher than for EM currencies. Let's assume it would cost 3.6% per year to maintain this strategy, which is three times higher than it is assumed for FX strategy. Contrary to EM FX, which lacks an obvious benchmark, JP Morgan's Emerging Market Bond Index (EMBI) is the clear choice for hard currency bonds. You can invest in the benchmark index through different forms such as total return swaps, ETF, and so on, which can be less expensive. Here let's assume the transaction cost for the benchmark EMBI is 1% per annum.

Fundamental Rules

The fundamental based investment strategy for emerging market hard currency bonds is similar to that for EM currencies. This simplified ranking system uses three macro-economic variables to determine the ranking of a country's ability to service its debt: GDP growth, debt to GDP, and inflation. The variables are slightly different than those used for currency. Note the exchange of short-term interest rates for debt to GDP. As holding a bond involves taking a credit risk, debt to GDP is particularly important to consider. Before making a loan to someone you have to determine their ability to repay, and as important as their income is you also need to consider their current outstanding debt in making that decision. As in the fundamental rules for currencies, this macro-economic data is available with a lag and is often subject to revision. To be conservative, the data from six months prior are used to determine the coming month's ranking. Table 3-6 documents the effectiveness of these three macro variables: Debt to GDP helps to increase the return compared to an equally weighted EM bond portfolio. Inflation helps to reduce the volatility but achieves lower overall return. GDP growth and debt to GDP help to increase return on a risk-adjusted basis (Sharpe ratio).

Combining all three fundamentals by simply averaging the rankings, the result is improved particularly on the risk side. Table 3-7 records the results: Annualized return is 6.4%, slightly higher than the 10-country equally weighted portfolio but lower than the broad EM bond index. Volatility, however, is the lowest compared with equally weighted portfolio and benchmark. Maximal one-month loss in 2008 is within the -10% mark, compared with the 16% loss from the EM bond index and the 14% loss from the equally weighted portfolio. On a risk-adjusted basis, it achieves a Sharpe ratio of 0.84, beating an equally weighted bond portfolio and three individual macro strategies, but not the broad EM bond index. In short, despite shrinking the investment universe to half by selecting only the top five fundamentally sound countries, this macro-based ranking system helps to reduce the risk but does not help to boost the return.

Table 3-6 Performance Statistics of Fundamental Ranking Rules for EM Hard Currency Bond Investment (January 2002–June 2013)

	\multicolumn{4}{c}{Average Annualized Return in %}	\multicolumn{4}{c}{Annualized Standard Deviation of Return in %}	\multicolumn{4}{c}{Sharpe Ratio}
	Eq. Weight	GDP	Debt to GDP	Inflation	Eq. Weight	GDP	Debt to GDP	Inflation	Eq. Weight	GDP	Debt to GDP	Inflation
2002-2007	5.61	6.54	6.23	3.68	10.07	9.40	10.51	7.52	0.56	0.70	0.59	0.49
2008	-5.93	-1.46	-5.62	-4.99	18.60	17.49	21.02	15.55	-0.32	-0.08	-0.27	-0.32
2009	16.61	14.06	17.55	15.67	6.55	6.94	7.11	6.47	2.54	2.03	2.47	2.42
2010-2013	-3.07	1.09	1.98	1.65	7.78	6.15	7.20	5.59	-0.39	0.18	0.28	0.30
Total	5.58	6.48	6.94	4.93	8.94	8.15	9.13	6.81	0.62	0.79	0.76	0.72

Source: Bloomberg, DataStream, IMF

Table 3-7 Performance Statistics of Combined Fundamental Ranking Rules for EM Hard Currency Bond Investment (January 2002–June 2013)

	Average Annualized Return in %				Annualized Standard Deviation of Return in %				Sharpe Ratio		
	Eq. Weight	Macro Strategy	EM Bond Index	Eq. Weight	Macro Strategy	EM Bond Index	Eq. Weight	Macro Strategy	EM Bond Index
2002-2007	5.61	7.00	7.56	10.07	6.33	7.04	0.56	1.10	1.07
2008	-5.93	1.67	-11.80	18.60	15.94	19.91	-0.32	0.10	-0.59
2009	16.61	11.88	25.61	6.55	8.51	7.09	2.54	1.40	3.61
2010-2013	-3.07	0.73	1.66	5.88	6.15	7.33	-0.52	0.12	0.23
Total	5.58	6.44	8.93	8.94	7.64	9.05	0.62	0.84	0.99

Source: Bloomberg, DataStream, IMF

Technical Rules

Sovereign CDS spread is the market's expectation of a country's credit worthiness. This is the forward-looking component based on the market's real-time gauge of a country's credit. As we did with currencies, to complement the macro ranking table, a CDS filtering rule can be applied to the bond investment universe. The CDS rule is that you buy only those bonds with a CDS spread that has not deteriorated more than a certain threshold over the past given month. Again, 20% is the threshold applied here. Be aware that this threshold does not maximize the return or Sharpe ratio over the particular sample period investigated. It is for illustrative purposes only and it is not a result of data mining.

From Table 3-8, you see the CDS filtering rule helps to increase the return to an annualized 9.1% and reduces the large losses occurred in 2008. Above all, maximal one-month loss is as low as 3.9%, less than half of that from the macro/fundamental strategy and only one-fourth the loss of the index. On a risk-adjusted basis, it possesses an attractive Sharpe ratio of 1.4, higher than the broad EM bond index.

Table 3-8 Performance Statistics of CDS Filtering Rule for EM Hard Currency Bond Investment (January 200–June 2013)

	Average Annualized Return in %			Annualized Standard Deviation of Return in %			Sharpe Ratio		
	Macro Strategy	CDS Filter	EM Bond Index	Macro Strategy	CDS Filter	EM Bond Index	Macro Strategy	CDS Filter	EM Bond Index
2002-2007	7.88	10.34	10.79	6.33	6.55	7.04	1.24	1.58	1.53
2008	1.67	7.85	-11.80	15.94	10.36	19.91	0.10	0.76	-0.59
2009	11.88	16.68	25.61	8.51	6.47	7.09	1.40	2.58	3.61
2010-2013	0.73	2.87	1.66	6.15	6.15	7.33	0.12	0.47	0.23
Total	6.44	9.12	8.93	7.64	6.71	9.05	0.84	1.36	0.99

Source: Bloomberg, DataStream, IMF

Combination of Macro Fundamentals and Market Indicator

Let's now combine the fundamental macro-economic based ranking system with the CDS filter. The investment strategy is the same as for currencies: Each month, you select the top five countries to invest according to their rankings in GDP, debt to GDP, and inflation and only buy those hard currency denominated sovereign bonds with a CDS spread that has not deteriorated more than 20% over the past month. Due to this rule, there will be months where you will want to buy the bonds of less than five countries. In this case you redistribute the risk to the remaining countries. At times you will want to be completely "risk off" from buying any EM bonds. If so, you would put the money into money markets.

One concern is that because the investment universe has shrunk to five countries or less, the resulting portfolio might be more volatile. The result recorded in Table 3-9 shows the contrary: Combining both the macro and the CDS filter, the portfolio achieves an average return, net transaction cost, of 9.3%. It is higher than the broad EM bond index (8.9%), higher than the 10-country equally weighted portfolio (5.6%), standalone macro/fundamental (6.4%), and slightly higher than CDS-based technical filter (9.1%). Compared with the broad EM bond benchmark, it achieved a higher Sharpe of 1.4 compared to 0.99 over the period of January 2002 to June 2013. The most desirable property of this rule based EM bond portfolio is its low maximal one-month loss. In 2008, the broad index lost 16% in one month, while a disciplined, rule based EM bond strategy suffered a loss as low as 3.4% during the global financial crisis. Risk adjusted cumulative returns are compared in Figure 3-5.

Table 3-9 Performance Statistics of Macro and CDS Joint Strategy for EM Hard Currency Bond Investment (January 2002 to June 2013)

	\multicolumn{3}{c}{Average Annualized Return in %}	\multicolumn{3}{c}{Annualized Standard Deviation of Return in %}	\multicolumn{3}{c}{Sharpe Ratio}
	Eq. Weight	Joint Rule	EM Bond Index	Eq. Weight	Joint Rule	EM Bond Index	Eq. Weight	Joint Rule	EM Bond Index
2002-2007	5.61	10.72	10.79	10.07	6.13	7.04	0.56	1.75	1.53
2008	-5.93	8.81	-11.80	18.60	11.8	19.91	-0.32	0.75	-0.59
2009	16.61	15.25	25.61	6.55	6.57	7.09	2.54	2.32	3.61
2010-2013	-3.07	2.66	1.66	7.78	5.90	7.33	-0.39	0.45	0.23
Total	5.58	9.33	8.93	8.94	6.67	9.05	0.62	1.40	0.99

Source: Bloomberg, DataStream, IMF

CHAPTER 3 • RULE BASED VALUE INVESTMENT   **143**

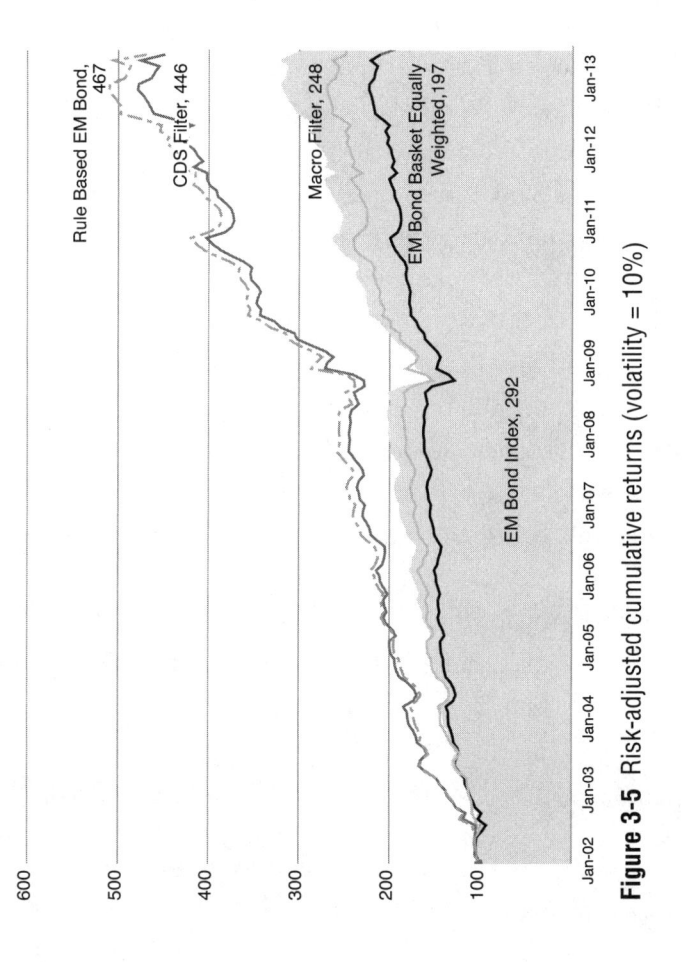

Figure 3-5 Risk-adjusted cumulative returns (volatility = 10%)

The examples reviewed here are extremely limited. The number of countries included in this EM investment example is small. In reality there are multiple emerging countries whose currencies are actively traded. JP Morgan's Emerging Markets Bond Index (EMBI) currently consists of 44 countries. This chapter serves as a basic walk-through meant to teach a framework and reveals the potential of basic rules. How to adjust these rules to maximize returns is another discussion. As recorded in Table 3-10, over the period of January 2002 to June 2013, this example rule based EM portfolio consisting of 50/50 emerging market foreign exchange strategy and emerging market bonds strategy achieved an annualized net return of 11.9%. This outperformed the stand-alone bond strategy (9.3%) and the broad EM bond index (8.9%) but underperformed the rule based EM FX strategy, which returned 14.3%. It outperformed other risky assets such as the S&P 500 and the Global High Yield Index. On the volatility front, rule based EM portfolio has an annualized standard deviation of less than 7% and maximal one-month loss of less than -6%. Therefore, on risk-adjusted basis, with a Sharpe ratio of 1.73, it outperforms a stand-alone rule based EM FX strategy, rule based bond strategy, as well as the broad EM bond index, meaning the "smartest investment" in terms of returns for the risk taken is the combined portfolio. The portfolio also outperformed other risky assets such as the S&P 500 and the Global High Yield Index from 2002 to June 2013, as show in Figure 3-6.

Table 3-10 Performance Statistics of Rule Based EM Currency and Bond Portfolio vs. Benchmark (January 2002 –June 2013)

	Average Annualized Return in %		Annualized Standard Deviation of Return in %		Sharpe Ratio	
	Rule Based EM Portfolio	*EM Bond Index*	*Rule Based EM Portfolio*	*EM Bond Index*	*Rule Based EM Portfolio*	*EM Bond Index*
2002-2007	15.18	10.79	5.39	7.04	2.82	1.53
2008	6.69	-11.80	9.59	19.91	0.70	-0.59
2009	21.88	25.61	9.65	7.09	2.27	3.61
2010-2013	2.54	1.66	6.72	7.33	0.38	0.23
Total	11.85	8.93	6.83	9.05	1.73	0.99

Source: Bloomberg, DataStream, IMF

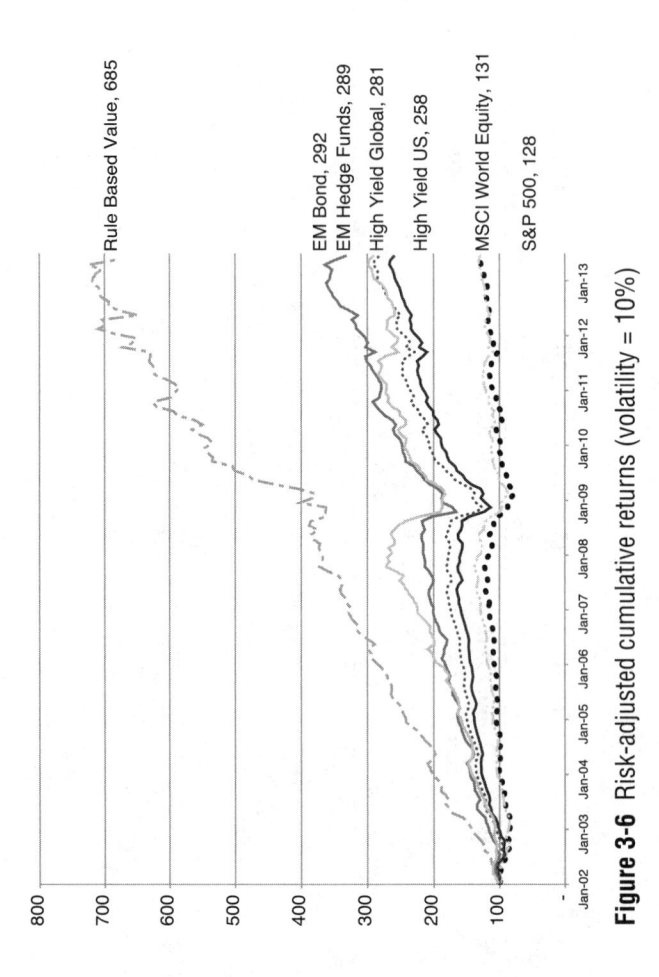

Figure 3-6 Risk-adjusted cumulative returns (volatility = 10%)

Some Remarks

There are numerous ways to improve the simple rule based strategies introduced in this chapter. In truth, professional investors specializing in emerging markets often employ much more complex models in attempt to capture higher returns. The rules introduced here, as with other chapters, are meant to serve as a "rule based benchmark" for demonstrating the sort of return/risk characteristic investors can potentially achieve through employing simple rules. These strategies are by no means written in stone, and the rules and parameters used here were not the result of data mining, but were chosen using knowledge derived from numerous academic research papers combined with extensive professional experience. Similar to how a chef might measure the ingredients of a dish by sight and touch alone, the rules and parameters chosen for this chapter, and this book, are drawn from past recipes for investment success.

Both the fundamental/backward looking and technical/forward looking aspect of this strategy can be refined and improved upon for superior returns. For example, many quantitative models incorporate credit ratings and many ratios have been used to better forecast the sovereign credit spread such as current account over GDP, reserves over imports, imports over GDP, real exchange rate, and so on. From the forward looking and technical side of this strategy, the VIX remains a valid risk indicator. There is also the TED Spread discussed earlier in the book, which can be used as an indicator of global liquidity. Correctly selecting and employing these more sophisticated indicators and other fundamental/historical data are subjects that must be discussed in greater depth in a future publication.

4

Rule Based Portfolio

In this book you have seen how to implement rule based investment strategies for several different asset classes, from foreign exchange to bonds and equity indices. Further, you've seen demonstrations of several different investment styles in volatility, carry, and value. The eclectic nature of these asset classes and investment styles is by design. Whereas many investment texts will narrow their focus on a single subject, the truth is no matter how great anyone's level of expertise in a single market, only diversification can offer relief from systemic and arbitrary market risks. Diversification requires uncorrelated investments, and uncorrelated investments in present times, require looking beyond stock and bond indices, toward emerging markets, toward volatility instruments, and toward currencies.

Typically investors are told over and over "invest in what you know," "buy and hold stocks over the long term," or "the S&P 500 is decent benchmark of returns," but by now the cumulative evidence presented should make you question these platitudes. Regarding international markets, "invest in what you know" is excessively conservative as typically your knowledge and experience is fairly limited. The truth is that at times, expertise is overrated. The 2008 crash is the sort of event that makes a fool of every expert. What is worse is that acquiring narrow market expertise is slow and inefficient because it is a skill that is nontransferrable across different subjects. The alternative of using general investment rules and principles that are applicable across markets will outperform "market expertise" in the long run.

Many investors struggle with true "diversification" because it requires building a portfolio that reflects the whole world: from European equities, to emerging market bonds, to interest rate volatility, and a wealth of other asset classes. Simple rules applied across a broad range of markets will produce a portfolio of diverse, robust, and, best of all, stable returns.

Now let's put everything together. Typically when you think of combining strategies you assume an equal weighting of each, but this is an overly simplistic method of allocation. Instead of equal weighting, a more intelligent approach is inverse, volatility weighting. Don't be intimidated, it is easy to implement by using a rolling 12-month standard deviation of each strategy's returns and allocating funds to each strategy inverse to its volatility. So if one strategy has low volatility, the next month's weighting will reflect a greater allocation to that strategy. If a strategy is increasingly volatile, the amount allocated will be reduced. The purpose of inverse volatility weighting is to minimize the variance of the sum, producing returns of greater stability.

This is the smarter way to allocate for superior returns for the amount of risk taken. Figure 4-1 records the resulting allocation over several years. Observe from the chart that weighting for the G10 carry trade has declined since 2007, the high water mark of the carry trade, although it now remains constant at around 20%. Allocation to the emerging market value investment exhibits cyclical movement with low weighting in 2012 and 2013. Volatility is dominant strategy in the years after 2007. In 2006, however, note that very little was allocated to volatility, the reason being the risk premium was low at the time.

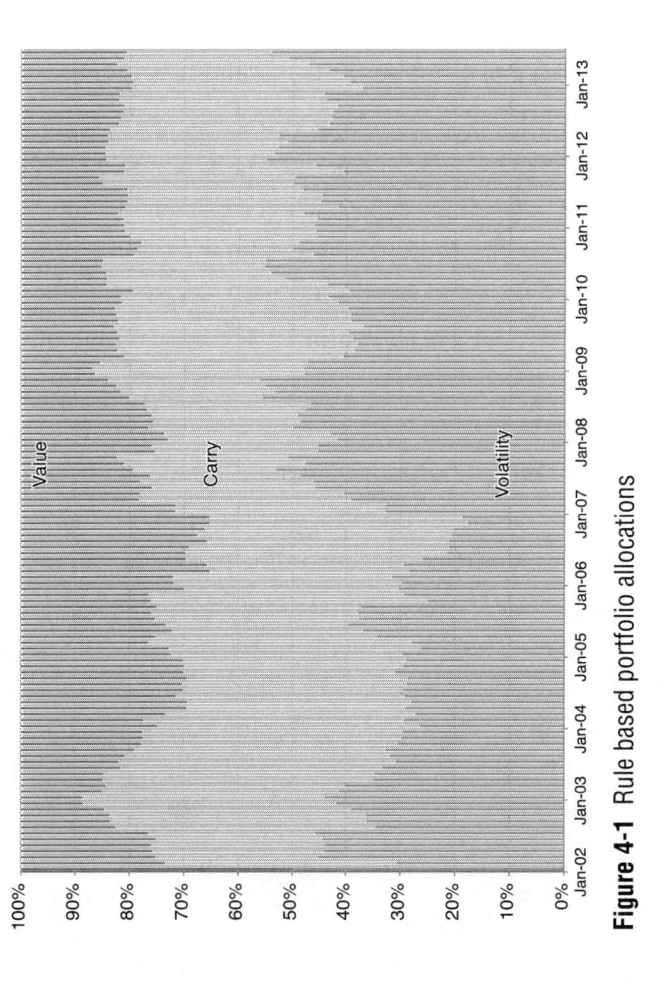

CHAPTER 4 • RULE BASED PORTFOLIO 151

Figure 4-1 Rule based portfolio allocations

Having allocated capital in this manner, it remains to discuss the results alongside traditional market benchmarks. The benchmarks used to compare the results of the rule based portfolio are two risky assets (S&P 500 and global high yield) as well as two indices representing the performance of professional money managers. One of these is the Barclay Systematic Trader Index, and the other one is Credit Suisse Dow Jones' Hedge Fund Index. The performance statistics of rule based investment strategies and benchmark indices are summarized in Table 4-1.

The first thing to note is that from Jan 2002 to June 2013, the stock market severely underperforms assets such as high yield and EM bonds. Not only did the S&P 500 produce the lowest returns of the assets compared here (~4.9%), its volatility was the highest, meaning great risk for meager returns. The global high yield index produced more than double the returns of the equity indices and with a superior risk profile as well.

It is worth noting that the professional money managers, on the average, did not outperform significantly the stock or high yield market indices. The Systematic Trader Index produced about the same return as the S&P 500 index, although the volatility of the returns is halved. The Hedge Fund Index had a lower volatility still and greater returns of just over 6%. Please note that the performance of rule based strategies are net of transaction costs; the systematic trader index and hedge fund index are net of fees; whereas benchmarks of equity and high yield are not.

Table 4-1 Performance Summary of Rule Based Investment Strategies vs. Benchmarks (January 2002–June 2013)

	Volatility Portfolio	Carry (G10) Portfolio	Value (EM) Portfolio	Rule Based Portfolio	S&P 500 Index	High Yield Global Index	Systematic Trader Index	Hedge Fund Index
Annualized Average Return in %								
2002–2007	11.62	3.70	15.18	11.27	4.81	10.96	5.67	9.90
2008	8.96	2.67	6.69	8.63	-45.45	-28.31	17.18	-20.53
2009	11.26	3.63	21.88	9.59	23.58	48.22	-3.29	17.26
2010–2013	12.31	4.07	2.54	9.82	13.09	9.05	0.10	5.75
Total	15.08	3.74	11.85	11.79	4.95	10.60	4.23	6.56
Annualized Return Standard Deviation in %								
2002–2007	4.47	3.15	5.39	3.00	11.51	6.84	9.04	3.80
2008	11.94	3.40	9.59	7.82	20.99	22.82	9.08	9.75
2009	10.04	4.46	9.65	5.03	22.31	12.43	5.58	4.71
2010–2013	9.20	3.78	6.72	5.14	15.77	8.60	6.37	4.96
Total	7.97	3.44	6.83	4.89	15.29	11.17	8.02	5.61
Sharpe Ratio								
2002–2007	2.60	1.18	2.82	3.76	0.42	1.60	0.63	2.61
2008	0.75	0.79	0.70	1.10	-2.17	-1.24	1.89	-2.11
2009	1.12	0.81	2.27	1.91	1.06	3.88	-0.59	3.66
2010–2013	1.34	1.07	0.38	1.91	0.83	1.05	0.02	1.16
Total	1.89	1.09	1.73	2.41	0.32	0.95	0.53	1.17

Source: Bloomberg

Figure 4-2 compares the risk/return profile of the rule based strategies with a broader category of benchmark indices. With the exception of rule based carry (which still outperforms the S&P 500 in Sharpe ratio), note how strong the returns of the ruled based value, rule based volatility, and the combined rule based portfolio are; the resulting return is multiples of the S&P 500, nearly double the returns of money managers. The volatility levels are competitive with and in the case of the combined portfolio, even lower than the Hedge Fund index. There exists tremendous potential because this portfolio achieved remarkable results and it is only the simplest case scenario. There is enormous room for improvement in refining and optimizing our strategies beyond the basics.

Figure 4-3 illustrates the cumulative returns with volatility normalized to 10% per year. The plotted lines speak for themselves. These results weren't achieved by whiz-kid financial wizardry, but rather by the systematic application of a simple framework of rules. The rules act as filters that take into account both historical information as well as forward-looking market sentiment. Tools such as GARCH use an intelligent average of historical prices, and in addition indicators such as the VIX alert us to market anxiety. The caution we should heed regarding these indicators is founded on a principle as basic as not flying a kite during a storm or cancelling a flight if there is a dense fog. The strategy is to take on positions that are long-term profitable, receiving volatility premium and receiving carry, and when uncertain times threaten, take risk off. Common sense and scientifically sound rules perform beautifully, particularly when emotions are removed from the investment process.

CHAPTER 4 • RULE BASED PORTFOLIO **155**

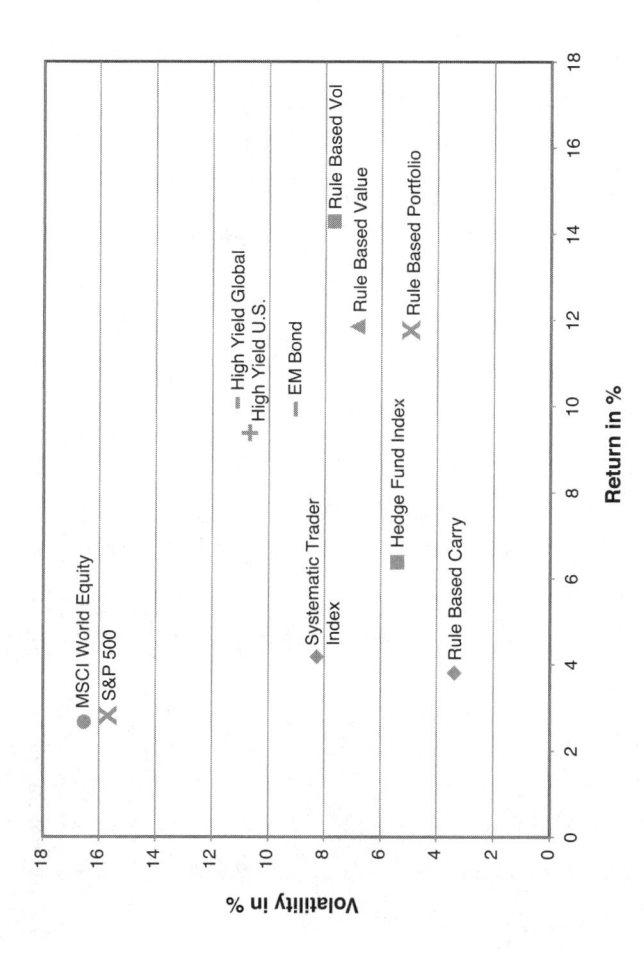

Figure 4-2 Risk/return comparisons

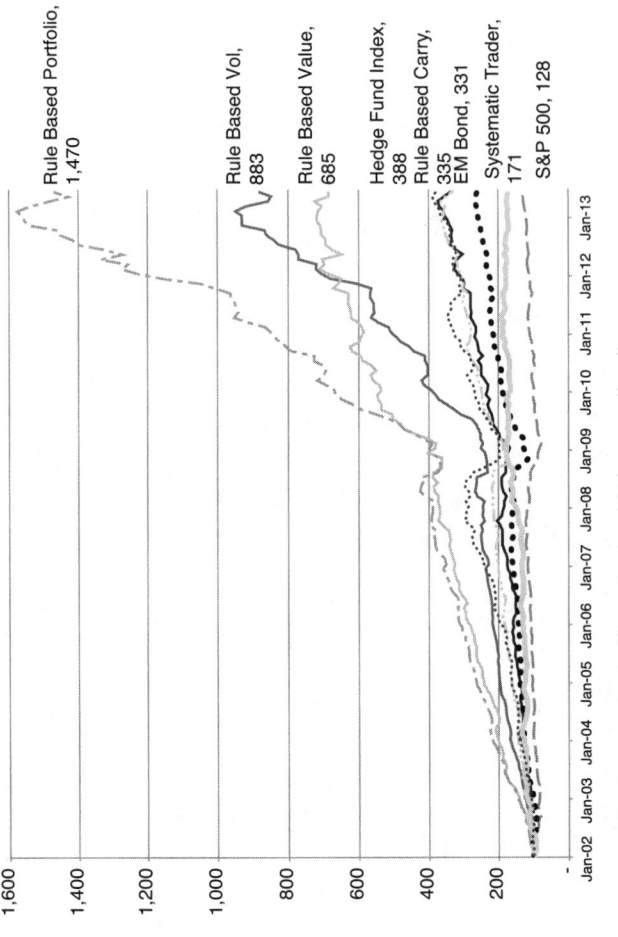

Figure 4-3 Cumulative returns (vol = 10% annualized)

Rule Based Portfolio, 1,470
Rule Based Vol, 883
Rule Based Value, 685
Hedge Fund Index, 388
Rule Based Carry, 335
EM Bond, 331
Systematic Trader, 171
S&P 500, 128

The Next Crisis and Beyond

An easy criticism to make of everything discussed so far is that no one has any way of knowing what will happen next in the markets. It might be that the next market crisis is unique in such a way that renders our strategies highly vulnerable. What is scientifically certain is that regardless of the next crisis, greater diversification is certain to spread out our risks and losses.

Skepticism is valued, but lazy skepticism is regressive. It is fact that past performance is not guarantee of future return, and tomorrow is an unknown for everyone. That the future is impossible to predict perfectly should not invalidate attempts to use salient principles from academia and market data to help us navigate the unfamiliar landscape of the future. The next crisis could be so severe no strategy is safe, but the answer is not to throw up our hands and give up on strategic investing. Rather, as we always have as a species, we will continue to learn and adapt from our failings as well as our successes.

The key lesson to take away from rule based strategies is that we can trust simple rules to take us far. Achieving strong stable returns does not require excessive complexity or a genius-level intellect, but rather the ability to apply basic rules in a regular and disciplined manner across diverse asset classes over the long term. Beware of "data mining" strategies that apply complicated rules to historical data to produce amazing simulated results. Be skeptical of complexity; it is essential to understand in simple terms how an investment makes money and why the opportunity persists. Throughout this book the examples have systematically shown investment in trades with persistent returns by applying filters that take into account basic historical information as well as forward-looking indicators. The key, then, is pursuing a combination of multiple simple strategies across eclectic asset classes to produce a basic but broadly diversified portfolio.

For discretionary investors, rule based strategies can offer excellent diversification. For systematic investors with "quant" backgrounds, this book has re-examined the first-principles that underlie and guide advanced strategies. For many others who have long been curious of what think tanks of Ph.D.s come up with on Wall Street, the strategies and ideas presented hopefully have been educational for you.

This book introduced the building blocks of rule based strategies. In truth it has examined only a limited number of asset classes and investing styles. Future publications will focus on other markets such as international equities and commodities to bring an ever greater diversity to an overall rule based portfolio. New strategies such as Global Macro will be introduced and advanced topics in momentum and volatility covered at greater length. This book has made a positive impact if the ideas and principles presented lead you and other readers to view investing from a new perspective—to think deeply of simple things. As the world becomes ever more complex and our professions increasingly specialized, a simple framework of investing rules applicable across markets will be ever more essential. As technological innovations continue to fuel profound social changes in an ever more complex and interconnected world, a future crisis is an inevitability. What is not inevitable is repeating the mistake of panicking; rule based investing offers a solution for making objective decisions under the difficult emotional circumstances of a crisis.

I hope you've found this accessible, and I hope the ideas presented shed light on the misunderstood field of quantitative or systematic investment. Typically people associate quant or rule based investing with high frequency trading, or they imagine a secret formula by market wizards that profits in all situations, but the truth is both more mundane and more remarkable. Mundane because the topics we've discussed are familiar and there is no bomb-shell secret to making money as an investor besides educated diversification into investments exhibiting persistent returns. What is remarkable is that intelligent diversification is possible though the application of a simple framework of rule based investing, and that with these rules, revisited on a monthly basis, even an individual investor is capable of professional returns. This book is intended to set the stage in introducing the principles of basic rule based systems across different markets. And if you have been paying attention there is every reason to be excited for what comes next, because if the basic "default" settings of the examples presented already produced enviable returns, imagine what is possible once our rules are refined. So, although we conclude here, truly this is only the beginning of understanding and mastering rule based investing. Thank you so much.

Bibliography

Ang, Andrew and Joseph S. Chen. "Yield Curve Predictors of Foreign Exchange Returns." Working Paper, 2010.

Baek, In-Mee, Arindam Bandopadhyaya, and Chan Du. "Determinants of Market-Assessed Sovereign Risk: Economic Fundamentals or Market Risk Appetite?" *Journal of International Money and Finance* 24 (June 2005): 533–548.

Bank for International Settlements, Triennial Central Bank Survey of Foreign Exchange and Derivatives Market Activity: 2001, 2004, 2007, and 2010.

Bansal, Ravi and Magnus Dahlquist. "The Forward Premium Puzzle: Different Tales from Developed and Emerging Economies." *Journal of International Economics, Elsevier* 51(1) (June 2000): 115–144.

Bernales, Alejandro and Massimo Guidolin. "Can We Forecast the Implied Volatility Surface Dynamics of Equity Options? Predictability and Economic Value Tests." Working Papers 456, IGIER (Innocenzo Gasparini Institute for Economic Research), Bocconi University, 2012.

Bhansali, Vineer. "Volatility and the Carry Trade." *The Journal of Fixed Income* 3 (Winter 2007): 72–84.

Bollerslev, Tim. "Generalized Autoregressive Conditional Heteroskedasticity." *Journal of Econometrics* 31 (April 1986): 307–327.

Bollerslev, Tim and Torben G. Andersen. "Heterogeneous Information Arrivals and Return Volatility Dynamics: Uncovering the Long-Run in High Frequency Returns." *Journal of Finance* 52 (3) (July 1997): 975–1005.

Bollerslev, Tim, George Tauchen, and Hao Zhou. "Expected Stock Returns and Variance Risk Premia." *Review of Financial Studies* 22 (11) (November 2009): 4463–4492.

Britten-Jones, Mark and Anthony Neuberger. "Option Prices, Implied Price Processes, and Stochastic Volatility." *Journal of Finance* 55 (April 2000): 839–866.

Brunnermeier, Markus K., Stefan Nagel and Lasse H. Pedersen. "Carry Trades and Currency Crashes." In *NBER Macroeconomics Annual 2008*. Vol. 23: National Bureau of Economic Research, Inc., 2009.

Burnside, Craig, Martin Eichenbaum, and Sergio Rebelo. "The Returns to Currency Speculation in Emerging Markets." *Review of Financial Studies* 24(3) (February 2007): 853–891.

Burnside, Craig. "Carry Trades and Risk." NBER Working Papers 17278, National Bureau of Economic Research, Inc. 2011.

Burnside, Craig, Martin Eichenbaum, and Sergio Rebelo. "Carry Trade and Momentum in Currency Markets." *Annual Review of Financial Economics, Annual Reviews* 3(1) (December 2011): 511–535.

Carr, Peter and Dilip Madan. "Towards a Theory of Volatility Trading." Chapter 29 in *Volatility: New Estimation Techniques for Pricing Derivatives*. London: Risk Books, 1998.

De Bock, Reinout and Irineu de Carvalho Filho. "The Behavior of Currencies During Risk-Off Episode." IMF Paper, 2013.

De Zwart, Gerben, ThijsMarkwat, Laurens Swinkels and Dick van Dijk. "The Economic Value of Fundamental and Technical Information in Emerging Currency Markets." *Journal of International Money and Finance* 28 (June 2009): 581–604.

Egloff, Daniel, Markus Leippold, and Liuren Wu. "The Term Structure of Variance Swap Rates and Optimal Variance Swap Investments." *Journal of Financial and Quantitative Analysis* 45(5) (October 2010): 1279–1310.

Engle, Robert. "Autoregressive Heteroscedasticity with Estimate of the Variance of United Kingdom Inflation." *Econometrica* 50 (4) (July 1982): 987–1008.

Frankel, Jeffrey and Jumana Poonawala. "The Forward Market in Emerging Currencies: Less Biased Than in Major Currencies." NBER Working Paper 12496, 2006.

Fama, Eugene F. and Kenneth R. French. "Dividend Yields and Expected Stock Returns." *Journal of Financial Economics* 22 (October 1988): 3–25.

Henry, Peter B. and Prakash Kannan. "Growth and Returns in Emerging Markets." In *International Financial Issues in the Pacific Rim: Global Imbalances, Financial Liberalization, and Exchange Rate Policy* Vol. 17, National Bureau of Economic Research, Inc., 2008.

Lustig, Hanno, Nikolai Roussanov and Adrien Verdelhan. "Common Risk Factors in Currency Markets." *Review of Financial Studies, Society for Financial Studies* 24 (11) (2011): 3731–3777.

Lustig, Hanno and Adrien Verdelhan. "The Cross-Section of Foreign Currency Risk Premia and Consumption Growth Risk: Reply." *American Economic Review* 101(7) (December 2011): 3477–3500.

Lustig, Hanno, Nikolai Roussanov, and Adrien Verdelhan. "Common Risk Factors in Currency Markets." *Review of Financial Studies* 24(11) (November 2011): 3731–3777.

Melvin, Michael and Mark P. Taylor. "The Crisis in the Foreign Exchange Market." *Journal of International Money and Finance* 28 (December 2009): 1317–1330.

Ranaldo, Angelo and Paul Söderlind. "Safe Haven Currencies." *Review of Finance, European Finance Association* 14(3) (March 2010): 385–407.

Reinhart, Carmen and Kenneth Rogoff. *This Time Is Different: Eight Centuries of Financial Folly*. Bew Herset: Princeton University Press, 2008.

Rennison, Graham and Niels Pedersen, "The Volatility Risk Premium," PIMCO Viewpoint (September 2012).

Ritter, Jay. "Is Economic Growth Good for Investors?" *Journal of Applied Corporate Finance* 24(3) (Summer 2012): 8–18.

Tuckman, Bruce and Angle Serrat. *Fixed Income Securities Tools for Today's Markets* 3rd ed. Wiley Finance, 2011.

Index

A

actual volatility, 16-17
   versus implied volatility, 20
allocation, rule based strategy, 150-154
applying filters
   GARCH filter
      applying to S&P 500 volatility strategy, 46-48
      applying to swap rates volatility, 58-60
      applying to USDJPY volatility strategy, 31-36
   joint GARCH/VIX filter
      applying to S&P 500 volatility strategy, 52
      applying to USDJPY volatility strategy, 41
   joint GARCH/vol curve filter, applying to swap rates volatility, 68-70
   VIX filter
      applying to carry investments, 96-103
      applying to S&P 500 volatility strategy, 48-52
      applying to USDJPY volatility strategy, 36-41
   volatility curve filter, applying to swap rates volatility, 63-66
AUDJPY versus risky assets, 89-92
avoiding risk in carry investments, market indicators, 96-103

B

Barclay Systematic Trader index, 69
benchmarks
   carry trade, 79
   performance of versus carry investments, 95-97
   returns in FX carry trades, 83-85
   volatility portfolio, building, 69-74
Big Mac index, 121
Black Scholes model, 9
bonds, 115
   value investing in sovereign bonds
      fundamental rules, 135-138
      technical rules, 139
Buffet, Warren, 89
building
   momentum strategy, 103-104
   volatility portfolio, 68-74
buy-and-hold strategy, 2, 26

C

capital markets, volatility, 13-17
  actual volatility, 16-17
  historical volatility, 16-17
  implied volatility, 16-17
  measuring, 13
  standard deviation, 13
  swap contracts, 14
capturing persistent returns, 4-5
carry trade, 79
  benchmark returns in FX carry trade, 83-85
  equally weighted carry basket, 99
  G10 carry basket, 92
  performance of versus benchmarks, 95-97
  risk of, 89-90
  risk-adjusted performance of currencies, 85-86
  rules for
    diversification, 94-97
    market indicators, reading, 96-103
    momentum strategy, 103-104
  Yen carry trade, 89-90
CDS (credit default swaps), 113-114
  combining with fundamental macro-economic based ranking, 141-144
  SCDS, 126-130
combining fundamental rules and risk indicators, 130-131
commodities, 9
credit worthiness of countries, measuring, 126-130
crisis events, effect on currencies, 122

currencies. *See also* currency markets
  effect of crisis events on, 122
  inflation, 122
  intrinsic value of, determining, 121
currency markets
  appreciation, 116-118
  buy-and-hold strategy, 83
  carry trade, 80
    benchmark returns in FX carry trade, 83-85
    equally weighted carry basket, 99
    G10 carry basket, 92
    momentum strategy, 103-104
    performance of versus benchmarks, 95-97
    risk-adjusted performance, 85-86
    rules for, 94-97
    Yen carry trade, 89-90
  debts, 134
  emerging market FX, rule based investment in, 118-119
  fundamental rule based strategy, ranking, 123-126

D

data mining strategies, 157
debts, 134
diversification
  for carry investments, 94-97
  general investment rules versus market expertise, 149
  inverse volatility weighting, 150-154

E

economic growth, effect on stock returns, 116
EM (emerging markets)
   CDS, 113-114
   debts, 134
   fundamental rules, combining with risk indicators, 130-131
   FX, rule based investment in, 118-119
   GDP, correlation to currency appreciation, 116-118
   macro fundamentals, combining with market indicators, 141-144
   SCDS, 126-130
   value investing, 109-114
      goals of, 112
      risks, 111
      in sovereign bonds,134-145
Engle, Robert, 17
equally weighted carry basket, 99
equity fund manager, selecting, 85
equity markets, S&P 500 volatility strategy, 44-52
   GARCH filter, applying, 46-48
examples of rule based volatility investments, 26-70
   S&P 500 volatility strategy, 44-52
      GARCH filter, applying, 46-48
      VIX filter, applying, 48-52
   swap rates volatilty, 55-70
      GARCH filter, applying, 58-60
      joint GARCH/vol curve filter, applying, 68-70
      volatility curve filter, applying, 63-66
   USDJPY rule based volatility strategy, 27-41
      GARCH filter, applying, 31-36
      VIX filter, applying, 36-39
expertise, investing in what you know, 149

F

fear of uncertainty, 25
Fed Funds Rates, 80
filters
   CDS filter, 126-130
      combining with fundamental macro-economic based ranking, 141-144
   GARCH filter
      applying to S&P 500 volatility strategy, 46-48
      applying to swap rates volatility, 58-60
      applying to USDJPY volatility strategy, 31-36
   joint GARCH/VIX filter
      applying to S&P 500 volatility strategy, 52
      applying to USDJPY volatility strategy, 41
   joint GARCH/vol curve filter
      applying to swap rates volatility, 68-70
   VIX filter
      applying to carry investments, 96-103
      applying to S&P 500 volatility strategy, 48-52
      applying to USDJPY volatility strategy, 36-41

volatility curve filter, applying to swap rates volatility, 63-66
forecasting, applying GARCH filter to rule based USDJPY volatility strategy, 31-36
fundamental rule based strategy
combining with risk indicators, 130-131
ranking, 123-126
value investing in sovereign bonds, 135-138
FX markets
carry trade
equally weighted carry basket, 99
momentum strategy, 103-104
performance of versus benchmarks, 95-97
risks of, 89-90
rules for, 94-97
Yen carry trade, 89-90
EM, rule based investment in, 118-119
equity fund manager, selecting, 85
fundamental rule based strategy, ranking, 123-126
rule based USDJPY volatility strategy, 27-41
GARCH filter, applying, 31-36

G

G10 carry basket, 92
GARCH filter
applying to S&P 500 volatility strategy, 46-48
applying to swap rates volatility, 58-60

applying to USDJPY volatility strategy, 31-36
GDP, correlation to currency appreciation, 116-118
Global Macro strategy, 158
goals of EM value investing, 112

H-I

hard currency denominated debt, 134
Hedge Fund Index, 152
historical volatility, 16-17
implied volatility, 10, 11, 16-17
versus actual volatility, 20
inflation, 122
insurance, 11
CDS, 113-114
interest rates
benchmark returns in FX carry trade, 83-85
Fed Funds Rates, 80
volatility, 57
inverse volatility weighting, 150-154
investing
quantitative investing, 159
uncorrelated investments, 149
value investing, 109-114
CDS, 113-114
EM, 109-114
in volatility portfolios, 71

J

joint GARCH/VIX filter
applying to S&P 500 volatility strategy, 52
applying to USDJPY volatility strategy, 41

joint GARCH/vol curve filter,
    applying to swap rates volatility,
    68-70

K-L

kurtosis profiles of currencies, 85
local currency denominated
    debt, 134

M

macro/fundamental ranking,
    126-131
market indicators, 19
    avoiding risk in carry investments,
        96-103
    combining with macro
        fundamentals, 141-144
    SCDS, 126-130
    TED spread, 103
measuring
    credit worthiness of countries,
        126-130
    volatility, 13
momentum strategy, building,
    103-104

N-O

naïve volatility strategy, 27
negative carry, 79
offshore trading, 116

P

performance of benchmarks versus
    carry investments, 95-97
persistent returns, capturing, 4-5

portfolio, building, 69-74
    inverse volatility weighting,
        150-154
positive carry, 79
PPP (purchasing power parity)
    rate, 115
profiting from volatility, 19-26
    fear of uncertainty, 25
    Sharpe ratio, 24

Q-R

quantitative investing, 159
ranking
    fundamental rule based strategy,
        123-126
    macro/fundamental ranking,
        126-130
risk premium, 11-13
risk-adjusted performance of
    currencies, 85-86
risks
    avoiding in carry investments,
        96-103
    combining with fundamental
        rules, 130-131
    in EM value investing, 111
    of FX carry trade, 89-90
    macro/fundamental ranking,
        126-130
rule based volatility investments
    examples, 26-70
        *rule based USDJPY volatility
        strategy, 27-41*

rule based USDJPY volatility strategy
   GARCH filter, applying, 31-36
   VIX filter, applying, 36-41
S&P 500 volatility strategy, 44-52
   GARCH filter, applying, 46-48
   VIX filter, applying, 48-52
swap rates volatilty, 55-70
   GARCH filter, applying, 58-60
   joint GARCH/vol curve filter, applying, 68-70
   volatility curve filter, applying, 63-66

S

S&P 500 volatility strategy, 44-52
   GARCH filter, applying, 46-48
   VIX filter, applying, 48-52
SCDS (Sovereign Credit Default Swap), 126-130
selecting an equity fund manager, 85
Sharpe ratio, 24
skew profiles of currencies, 85
sovereign bonds, value investing, 134-145
   fundamental rules, 135-138
   technical rules, 139
speculators, 10-11
standard deviation, 13
statistics, 19
stocks, 9
   economic growth, effect on returns, 116

EM
   goals, 112
   risks, 111
   value investing, 109-114
value investing, 109-114
variance of prices, 33
straddle, 44
swap contracts, 14
   CDS, 113-114
swap rates volatilty, 55-70
   GARCH filter, applying, 58-60
   joint GARCH/vol curve filter, 68-70
   volatility curve filter, applying, 63-66
Systematic Trader Index, 152

T

technical rules, value investing in sovereign bonds, 139
TED spread, 103
treasuries, 9

U

uncertainty
   fear of, 25
   VIX filter
      applying to carry investments, 96-103
      applying to S&P 500 volatility strategy, 48-52
      applying to USDJPY volatility strategy, 36-41
uncorrelated investments, 149
U.S. Federal Reserve, Fed Funds Rates, 80

USDJPY rule based volatility strategy, 27-41
   GARCH filter, applying, 31-36
   VIX filter, applying, 36-39

V

value investing, 109-114
   CDS, 113-114
   in emerging markets, 109-114
      GDP, correlation to currency appreciation, 116-118
      goals of, 112
      risks, 111
      sovereign bonds, 134-145
variance
   of stock prices, 33
   swap contracts, 14
VIX filter
   applying to carry investments, 96-103
   applying to S&P 500 volatility strategy, 48-52
   applying to USDJPY volatility strategy, 36-41
volatility, 9
   actual volatility, 16-17
   in capital markets, 13-17
   examples of rule based volatility investments, 26-70
      rule based USDJPY volatility strategy, 27-41
   Hedge Fund Index, 152
   historical volatility, 16-17
   implied volatility, 10, 11, 16-17
   interest rates, 57
   inverse weighting, 150-154
   investing in through rules, 17-19
      market indicators, 19
      statistics, 19
   measuring, 13
   naïve volatility strategy, 27
   profiting from, 19-26
      fear of uncertainty, 25
      Sharpe ratio, 24
   risk premium, 11-13
   swap contracts, 14
   swap rates volatility, applying GARCH filter, 58-60
volatility curve filter, applying to swap rates volatility, 63-66
volatility portfolio, building, 69-74

W-X-Y-Z

Yen carry trade, 89-90